The
Greek
Paradox

Promise vs.
Performance

CSIA Studies in International Security

Michael E. Brown, Sean M. Lynn-Jones, & Steven E. Miller, series editors
Teresa J. Lawson, executive editor
Center for Science and International Affairs (CSIA)
John F. Kennedy School of Government, Harvard University

Published by The MIT Press:

The International Dimensions of Internal Conflict, Michael E. Brown, ed. (1996)

Avoiding Nuclear Anarchy: Containing the Threat of Loose Russian Nuclear Weapons and Fissile Material, Graham T. Allison, Owen R. Coté, Jr., Richard A. Falkenrath, and Steven E. Miller (1996)

The Arms Production Dilemma: Contraction and Restraint in the World Combat Aircraft Industry, Randall Forsberg, ed. (1994)

Shaping Europe's Military Order: The Origins and Consequences of the CFE Treaty, Richard A. Falkenrath (1994)

Published by Brassey's, Inc.:

Damage Limitation or Crisis? Russia and the Outside World, Robert D. Blackwill and Sergei A. Karaganov, eds. (1994)

Arms Unbound: The Globalization of Defense Production, David Mussington (1994)

Russian Security After the Cold War: Seven Views from Moscow, Teresa Pelton Johnson and Steven E. Miller, eds. (1994)

Published by CSIA:

Cooperative Denuclearization: From Pledges to Deeds, Graham Allison, Ashton B. Carter, Steven E. Miller, and Philip Zelikow, eds. (1993)

Soviet Nuclear Fission: Control of the Nuclear Arsenal in a Disintegrating Soviet Union, Kurt M. Campbell, Ashton B. Carter, Steven E. Miller, and Charles A. Zraket (1991)

The Greek Paradox

Promise vs. Performance

Editors
Graham T. Allison
& Kalypso Nicolaïdis

The MIT Press
Cambridge, Massachusetts
London, England

#35658069

© 1997 by the Center for Science and International Affairs
John F. Kennedy School of Government
Harvard University
Cambridge, Massachusetts 02138
(617) 495-1400

Library of Congress Cataloging-in-Publication Data

The Greek paradox: promise vs. performance / editors, Graham T. Allison & Kalypso Nicolaïdis.
  p. cm.—(CSIA studies in international security)
Includes index.
ISBN 0-262-51092-8 (pbk.: alk. paper)
1. Greece—Politics and government—1974– . 2. Greece—Relations—Balkan Peninsula. 3. Balkan Peninsula—Relations—Greece. 4. Greece—Foreign relations—1974– . 5. Political stability—Greece. I. Allison, Graham T. II. Nicolaïdis, Kalypso. III. Series.
   DF854.G745 1996
949.507'6—dc20   96-46473
                         CIP

Editing, indexing, and desktop publishing by Lynne Meyer-Gay
Design by Miriam Avins and Lynne Meyer-Gay

10 9 8 7 6 5 4 3 2 1
Printed in the United States of America

Contents

Tables
& Figures

This volume is dedicated to the leaders and citizens of Greece. May they seize the significant opportunities before them and inspire the spirit of democracy around the world not only by their history but by their performance.

Contributors

Graham T. Allison is Douglas Dillon Professor of Government and Director of the Center for Science and International Affairs at Harvard University's John F. Kennedy School of Government, where he was Dean from 1977–89. Allison's recent research and teaching has examined the former Soviet Union and American foreign and defense policy. He founded the Strengthening Democratic Institutions Project and drafted, with Grigory Yavlinsky, "The Window of Opportunity," a plan for Western engagement in the Soviet transition to democracy and a market economy. His concept of a "Grand Bargain" was first presented in a *Foreign Affairs* article (Spring 1991), co-authored with Robert Blackwill. His first book, *Essence of Decision*, approaching its 25th anniversary in 1996, articulates two theoretical paradigms to compete with the "rational actor" model that had previously dominated foreign policy analysis. Dr. Allison is co-editor of *Fateful Visions* (1988); *Hawks, Doves, and Owls: An Agenda for Avoiding Nuclear War* (1985); and, more recently, co-author of *Avoiding Nuclear Anarchy: Containing the Threat of Loose Russian Nuclear Weapons and Fissile Material* (1996). Prior to his current role as CSIA's director, he served as Assistant Secretary of Defense for Policy and Plans, coordinating DOD strategy towards the states of the former Soviet Union. He continues to serve as Special Advisor to Secretary of Defense William Perry and has been a member of the Defense Policy Board for Secretaries Weinberger, Carlucci, Cheney, Aspen, and Perry.

Gianna Angelopoulos-Daskalaki is Vice Chairman of the Dean's Council of the John F. Kennedy School of Government at Harvard University. She studied law at the University of Thessaloniki and practiced as a lawyer in Athens after graduating. In 1986, she became actively involved in politics and was elected City Councilor of the Athens Municipality. She was elected Deputy to the Greek Parliament in November 1989 and reelected in April 1990. Mrs.

Angelopoulos-Daskalaki was recently appointed by the Prime Minister of Greece to serve as President of the "Athens 2004" Olympic bid committee. She is married to Theodore Angelopolous, a major Greek industrialist, and is active in their shared international business interests.

P. Nikiforos Diamandouros is Professor of Political Science at the University of Athens. He serves as Director-Chairman of the National Centre for Social Research (EKKE) in Greece and President of the Greek Political Science Association. He is former Program Director for Western Europe and the Near and Middle East for the Social Science Research Council (SSRC), and former Director of the Greek Institute for International and Strategic Affairs. He holds M.A. and Ph.D. degrees in political science from Columbia University and is a recipient of National Endowment for the Humanities and Fulbright grants. Currently, he is Joint General Editor of the SSRC Series on the New Southern Europe (Johns Hopkins University Press). His research concentrates on the politics and history of Greece and southern Europe, and he has published widely on issues of democratization, state formation and nation building, and cultural change in the aforementioned areas. Dr. Diamandouros has published widely, in many languages. He is coeditor of *The Politics of Democratic Consolidation: Southern Europe in Comparative Perspective* (1995); he is author of "Prospects for Democracy in the Balkans: Comparative and Theoretical Perspective," in F. Stephen Larrabee, ed., *The Volatile Powder Keg: Balkan Security after the Cold War* (1994); *Cultural Dualism and Political Change in Postauthoritarian Greece* (1994); "Transition to, and Consolidation of, Democratic Politics in Greece, 1974–83," in Geoffrey Pridham, ed., *The New Mediterranean Democracies* (1987); and "La transicion del autoritarismo a la democracia en Grecia," in Julian Santamaria, ed., *Transicion a la democracia en el sur de Europa y America Latina* (1982).

Michael S. Dukakis is former Governor of Massachusetts and currently Professor of Political Science at Northeastern University. He is a graduate of Swarthmore College and Harvard Law School. He began his political career as an elected town meeting member of Brookline, Massachusetts. He was elected Chairman of his town's Democratic organization in 1960 and won a seat in the Massachusetts legislature in 1962, serving four terms. Dukakis was elected governor of Massachusetts in 1974 and again in 1982, after a term out of office. He was reelected for an unprecedented third term in 1986 by one of the largest margins in history. In 1986, his colleagues in the National Governors' Association voted him the most effective governor in the nation. Dukakis became the Democratic nominee for president of the United States in 1988 and was defeated by George Bush. Soon thereafter, he announced that he would not be a candidate for reelection as governor and served his final two years as governor in a time of increasing financial and economic distress in Massachusetts and the Northeast. Since June 1991, in addition to teaching at Northeastern University, he has taught in the Senior Executive Program for State and Local Managers at Harvard University's John F. Kennedy School of Government. He has also been Visiting Professor at Florida Atlantic University, the University of Hawaii, and the University of California at Los Angeles.

Misha Glenny is a writer and a journalist, covering Eastern Europe and the former Yugoslavia for over ten years as a correspondent for the *Guardian* and the British Broadcasting Company. He has contributed to many publications, including *The New York Times, The New York Review of Books, Harper's Magazine,* and *The New Yorker.* He is the author of two books: *The Rebirth of History: Eastern Europe in the Age of Democracy* and *The Fall of Yugoslavia: The Third Balkan War.* As a fellow of the Woodrow Wilson Center for International Scholars in Washington, D.C., he is currently writing a book about the rise of Balkan national consciousness and the great powers. Mr. Glenny is a fellow of the World Economic Forum and has been selected as the Fulbright Distinguished Guest to address the 1996 meeting of the American Historical Association.

Dimitris Keridis is Research Associate at the Institute for Foreign Policy Analysis, Cambridge, and a doctoral candidate of international relations at the Fletcher School of Law and Diplomacy, Tufts University. He is a graduate of the School of Law at the University of Thessaloniki and the Law Academy of the European University Institute in Florence, and holds an M.A.L.D. degree from the Fletcher School. His main academic interests are European integration, Balkan security, and theories of international relations and conflict resolution. He has been awarded numerous scholarships and research grants by U.S. and European institutions. His publications include book reviews and short papers on the post-communist Balkans.

F. Stephen Larrabee is a senior staff member at RAND in Santa Monica, California. He previously served as Vice President and Director of Studies at the Institute for East-West Security Studies in New York. From 1978 to 1981, he was a member of the National Security Council staff, dealing with Soviet and East European affairs. He has also held teaching positions at Cornell, Columbia, New York, and Georgetown Universities, The Johns Hopkins School of Advanced International Studies (SAIS), and the University of Southern California. Dr. Larrabee has published widely on East-West relations, especially the Balkans. His most recent books include *The Volatile Powder Keg: Balkan Security after the Cold War* (ed., 1994); *East European Security after the Cold War* (1994); *Conventional Arms Control and East-West Security* (with Robert Blackwill, 1989); and *The Two German States and European Security* (1989). He is also the author of "Long Memories and Short Fuses: Change and Instability in the Balkans," published in *International Security* (Winter 1990/91); and "Balkan Security," an International Institute for Strategic Studies *Adelphi Paper* (1976).

Kalypso Nicolaïdis is Assistant Professor of Public Policy at the John F. Kennedy School of Government, Harvard University, teaching courses on negotiation, international institutions, and the European Community. She also teaches a yearly seminar on international negotiations and conflict resolution at the École Nationale d'Administration in Paris. She holds an M.A. degree in international economics from the Institut d'Études Politiques in Paris, an M.P.A. from the Kennedy School, and a Ph.D. in political economy and government from Harvard's departments of economics and government. In her research, she combines long-standing interests in exploring the sources of cooperation in regional and multilateral settings, the role of ideas in international relations, and the dynamics of bargaining under conditions of complexity. Her current work concerns the post–Uruguay Round agenda, and United Nations reform, including the area of preventive diplomacy. She is also completing a book on the principle of mutual recognition in the European Community. Dr. Nicolaïdis has previously published work on the European Community, Eastern Europe, and the GATT, and is the editor of *Strategic Trends in Services: An Enquiry into the*

World Services Economy. She has worked in or with several international institutions, including OECD, GATT, UNCTAD, IIASA, and the EU, and is currently Chairman of Services World Forum. She is a faculty associate of Harvard University's Center for International Affairs and Center for European Studies.

Joseph S. Nye, Jr. is Don K. Price Professor of Public Policy at Harvard University and Dean of the John F. Kennedy School of Government. He served as Assistant Secretary of Defense for International Security Affairs until December 1995. A 1958 graduate of Princeton University and a Rhodes Scholar, he earned his Ph.D. from Harvard in 1964 and joined the faculty shortly thereafter. He was awarded tenure as a professor of government in 1971 and later held named chairs in the Faculty of Arts and Sciences and the Kennedy School of Government. A seasoned administrator, Dr. Nye served as Director of the Center for Science and International Affairs (CSIA) from 1985 to 1990, as Associate Dean of the Faculty of Arts and Sciences from 1989 to 1992, and as Director of Harvard University's Center for International Affairs (CFIA) from 1989 to 1994. He has taught core courses in foreign affairs at both the Kennedy School and Harvard College. His many publications include *Nuclear Ethics* (1986), *Bound to Lead: The Changing Nature of American Power* (1990), and *Understanding International Conflicts* (1993).

Alexis Papahelas is U.S. correspondent for Greek MEGA Television Channel, *Kathimerini* daily, and Washington correspondent for the BBC World Service–Greek Program. He holds an M.A. degree in international affairs from Columbia University and a B.A. from Bard College. He has lectured at Columbia, Yale, and American Universities, the Foreign Service Institute, and other forums in the United States and Greece. Among his productions are "The U.S. Role in the 1967 Coup in Greece," a documentary produced for MEGA Channel, and "The Turkish Invasion of Cyprus in 1974: The U.S. Role."

Elizabeth Prodromou is Visiting Lecturer in the Department of Politics at Princeton University, where she has been appointed Assistant Professor at the Woodrow Wilson School of Public and International Affairs (1995–96). She holds Ph.D. and S.M. degrees in political science from the Massachusetts Institute of Technology, an M.A.L.D. degree from the Fletcher School of Law and Diplomacy, and a B.A. in international relations and history from Tufts

University. Her research focuses on southeastern Europe and Greek-Turkish relations, with concentration on nationalism and ethnic conflict management, democratization and religious transformation, and state legitimacy. Her publications include "Democratic Consolidation and Religious Change in the New Southern Europe: Spain, Portugal, Italy, Greece" (with Jose Casanova), in *Democracy and Culture Change in the New Southern Europe* (Spring 1997); "Paradigms, Power and Identity: Rediscovering Religion and Regionalizing Europe," *European Journal of Political Research* (Fall 1996); "Orthodoxy, Nationalism and Political Culture in Contemporary Greece" (in Greek), *Greek Review of Political Science* (April 1995); and "Towards an Understanding of Eastern Orthodoxy and Democracy Building in the Post–Cold War Balkans," *Mediterranean Quarterly* (Spring 1994).

Monteagle Stearns served as U.S. Ambassador to Greece from 1981 to 1985. As a career foreign service officer, he was also U.S. Ambassador to the Republic of Ivory Coast from 1976 to 1979 and Vice President of the National Defense University from 1979 to 1981. Since leaving the foreign service in 1987, he has been Fellow at the Woodrow Wilson International Center for Scholars in Washington, D.C.; Warburg Professor of International Relations at Simmons College in Boston; Whitney H. Shepardson Fellow at the Council on Foreign Relations in New York; and an associate and affiliate of the Center for International Affairs (CFIA) at Harvard University. In 1992, his book *Entangled Allies: U.S. Policy toward Greece, Turkey and Cyprus* was published by the Council on Foreign Relations. A Greek edition was published the same year by PONTIKI press in Athens. Ambassador Stearns recently completed a book on American diplomacy for the 20th Century Fund, entitled *Talking to Strangers: Improving American Diplomacy at Home and Abroad* (1996).

Constantine Stephanopoulos is President of the Republic of Greece, elected by the Greek Parliament on March 8, 1995. He studied law at the University of Athens and began his law practice in Patras in 1954. He has been active in politics for thirty years. His political career began in 1964, when he was elected to the Greek Parliament from the prefecture of Achaia as a member of the National Radical Union (ERE) party. He was reelected in 1974, 1977, 1981, and 1985, from Achaia, as a member of the Nea Demokratia (New

Democracy) party. In 1989, as a member of DHANA, he was elected to the Greek Parliament from the greater Athens area. In June 1994, following the European elections, he dissolved the DHANA party and withdrew from politics. During his political career, President Stephanopoulos has served as Undersecretary to the Ministry of Commerce (July 1974 to November 1974), Minister of the Interior (November 1974 to September 1976), Minister of Social Services (September 1976 to November 1977), and Advisor to the Prime Minister (November 1977 to October 1981).

Stavros B. Thomadakis is Professor of Financial Economics at the University of Athens. He is the author of several books and many scholarly articles on financial and industrial economics, banking, and economic history. In 1993 he co-edited (with Harry Psomiades) a collection of essays entitled *Greece, the New Europe, and the Changing International Order.* He has served on the Greek Council of Economic Advisors, the Monetary Committee of the European Community, and bank boards of directors. He was a member of the "Angelopoulos Committee on the State of the Greek Economy" in 1990. He has also served as Chairman of the Board of the Greek Center for Economic Research (KEPE), and is now Chairman of the Capital Market Commission of Greece.

Basilios E. Tsingos is Lecturer on Social Studies at Harvard University, where he teaches courses on the theory and history of European integration and modern Greek political history. He received his A.B. degree from Harvard in 1990 and attended Oxford University as a Rhodes Scholar, where he received both M.Phil. and D.Phil. degrees in international relations. His dissertation, entitled "Underwriting Democracy, Not Exporting It: The European Community and Greece," was nominated by Oxford for the Lord Bryce Prize in International Relations, awarded by the British Political Science Association. He is the author of papers in *Harvard Journal of Law and Public Policy* and in Laurence Whitehead, ed., *The International Dimensions of Democratization: Europe and the Americas* (1996). He has worked for the U.S. Department of State, Michael Heseltine in the British House of Commons, and the law firm of Hale and Dorr. He currently is Clerk to the Hon. Norman Stahl of the U.S. Circuit Court of Appeals for the First Circuit.

Loukas Tsoukalis is Jean Monnet Professor of European Integration at the University of Athens, Professor and Director of the Economics

Department at the College of Europe in Bruges, and Chairman of Synthesis (European Studies, Research and Strategy) in Athens, Greece. He holds a B.A. degree from the University of Manchester, a Diplôme de Hautes Études Européennes from the College of Europe in Bruges, and an M.A. and D.Phil. degree from Oxford University. Among the many positions he has held are President of the Administrative Council and Director of the Hellenic Center for European Studies (EKEM), University Lecturer in International Relations and Fellow of St. Antony's College at Oxford, and Ambassador and Special Advisor for European Community Affairs to the prime minister of Greece during Greece's presidency of the European Community in the 1980s. Dr. Tsoukalis has been a member of the editorial board of *International Organization* and editor and member of the editorial board of the *Journal of Common Market Studies*. His extensive publications in international political economy and European financial integration include *The New European Economy* (1993), *The European Community and Its Mediterranean Enlargement* (1981), and *The Politics and Economics of European Monetary Integration* (1977).

Susan L. Woodward is Senior Fellow at the Brookings Institution. She holds M.A. and Ph.D. degrees in political science from Princeton University, and a B.A. from the University of Minnesota. She has been head of the Analysis and Assessment Unit in the Office of the Special Representative of the Secretary General in UNPROFOR Headquarters in Zagreb; Associate Professor of Political Science at Yale University; Assistant Professor at Williams College, Mount Holyoke College, and Northwestern University; and has taught most recently at Georgetown and George Washington Universities. She has earned numerous scholarly and teaching awards and honors. Dr. Woodward is the author of *Balkan Tragedy: Chaos and Dissolution after the Cold War* (1995); and *Socialist Unemployment: The Political Economy of Yugoslavia, 1945–90* (1995).

Preface

Gianna
Angelopoulos-
  Daskalaki
&
Graham T.
Allison

The title of this volume mirrors that of the special Harvard Leadership Symposium we convened and co-chaired in October 1995. In choosing the title, we meant to be provocative. "The Greek Paradox: Promise vs. Performance"—the oft-noted gap between Greece's unlimited promise and its sometimes disappointing performance—is simultaneously disturbing, intriguing, and instructive.

The birthplace of democracy finds itself with a government that is often paralyzed. How can this be? and how can this be overcome? Economically—in entrepreneurship, finance, shipping, and business—individual Greeks push the frontiers of the global economy, while Greece itself lags behind other member countries in the European Union. Why? and what can be done to accelerate Greece's economic performance? Geopolitically, a nation that should serve as a natural hub of the Balkans and a pillar of stability in a volatile region repeatedly falls victim to insecurities that prevent realization of its potentialities. Once again, why? and what can be done to enhance Greece's security and the security of other countries of the region?

To address the issue of the Greek Paradox, we commissioned papers by four leading Greek and American analysts of Greece's politics, economics, and security. With these papers as a starting point, we convened a diverse cross section of Greek and American academics, politicians, journalists, and business leaders. We asked them to address our objectives in this enterprise and to answer two questions: What are the principal causes of the observed gap between Greece's promise and its performance? What specific actions can be taken to narrow this gap—what actions by government, or politicians, or business leaders, or citizens, or other governments, or friends?

President Constantine Stephanopoulos of Greece honored our symposium by presenting the opening address in the Forum of Harvard's John F. Kennedy School of Government. He challenged participants to be bold in thinking about agendas for action. Our sessions included long-time American friends of Greece, including

Ambassadors John Kenneth Galbraith and Monteagle Stearns, and prominent Greek Americans like Michael Dukakis, whose perspective on Greek-American politics forms one of the book's most interesting chapters.

The diversity of the participants and the relevance of the topic stimulated lively and heated debate. The sessions were not arduously abstract or theoretical; they brimmed with passion, vehemence, and spirit. In selecting nontraditional participants with unique styles, perspectives, and expertise, we sought to reflect the varied forces influencing Greece today. In many ways, we succeeded.

Our deliberations and progression toward an agenda for the future were not linear. They exemplified what the chapters of this volume explain clearly—the realization of Greece's performance will require many long-term and difficult social, structural, and psychological adaptations. The good news from the symposium, we believe, is reflected in these chapters and in Loukas Tsoukalis's conclusion that summarizes the best from the discussions. That message is the growing realism—apparent across the spectrum of Greek leadership—about Greece's predicament and the objective conditions that narrow the margins for choice by Greek governments, Greek businesses, and Greek citizens. Greece's geopolitical location, the conditions for its participation in the European Union, and its integration into the global economy pose demanding, inescapable challenges that increasingly narrow its freedom of action. Paradoxically, the tightening of external constraints sometimes acts as the mother of creativity in the renewal and reform of Greece's economy, society, and polity. In scrutinizing Greece's challenges, the extraordinary opportunities for both internal and regional leadership become clear. Whether Greeks and friends of Greeks step up to these challenges and opportunities remains to be seen. But based on the evidence of this symposium and its participants, we report considerable grounds for optimism.

The focus of this volume is Greece, but the lessons of the Greek Paradox and the agendas for action to narrow the gap reach beyond Greece to most societies on the globe today. Everywhere governments are failing, or seen to fail. Weak governments, divided governments, tarnished leaders, quarrelsome and disappointed citizens—none are unique to Greece. Particularly in an era of democratization, where over the past decade more than thirty nations in the former Soviet Union, Central and Eastern Europe, Latin America, Africa, and East Asia have adopted structures of constitutional democracy and chosen leaders by free elections, many are tempted to euphoria over the arrival of the apparent solution to all problems, or as one scholar has argued, the "end of history." But examining in detail the fabric of the first democracy, one is reminded of the wisdom of Winston Churchill's observation: democracy is the worst form of government known to man—except for all the others. Indeed, Greek democracy, American democracy, as well as newly-established democracy in new states, remain and will continue to remain works in progress. Revising citizens' unrealistic expectations about promise on the one hand, and achieving the high and quite realistic possibilities for performance on the other, requires continuous vigilance and exertion by leaders in every society. Our hope and expectation is that this initial symposium has been a first step toward an ongoing collaboration between Harvard University and a diverse cross-section of Greek leadership on these profound challenges to Greece and to other nations of the world.

This volume, and the symposium on which it is based, had its origins in the mind of one of us—Gianna Angelopoulos-Daskalaki. She and her husband, Theodore Angelopoulos, a distinguished Greek businessman, recognized the need for such a dialogue to occur, preferably under Harvard's auspices, where both neutrality and expertise could be deployed. Their ideas struck a responsive chord in the co-chair, Graham Allison, who marshaled Harvard resources to make the idea a reality. We had the pleasure of collaborating not only in the conception, but also in the conduct of the symposium. We look forward to a continuing collaboration, building on the foundation laid here.

Neither the symposium nor this book would have been possible without the energy and support of many individuals, including the co-editor of the volume, Kalypso Nicolaïdis; Holly Sargent, Associate Dean of the Kennedy School, and members of her staff; Sean Lynn-Jones and Teresa Lawson, who provided editorial advice; Loukas Tsoukalis, who helped us bridge the American-Greek expanse; and Dimitris Keridis, whose efforts helped make the symposium a success. Finally, this project would not have been possible without the sharp editorial eye and tireless commitment of Lynne Meyer-Gay, who is reported to have become in the process Greek by adoption.

— Graham T. Allison
— Gianna Angelopoulos-Daskalaki
August 1996

The Greek Paradox

Promise vs. Performance

Chapter 1

Kalypso Nicolaïdis

Introduction: What is the Greek Paradox?

The Achilles [paradox] ... affirms that even the runner most famed for his speed must fail in his pursuit of the slowest.
Aristotle, Physics, Book VI.9.

Is there a Greek paradox? Contributors to this book believe that there is a paradox of modern Greece worth analyzing, even if they disagree on why it came about and what is to be done about it. By entitling the project in this way, we do not seek to be gratuitously provocative. To suggest that Greece's performance today does not match its promise should be understood as a call to arms, not a cause for despair. Indeed, our diagnosis should not be confused with the mind-set shared by nostalgic philhellenes around the world, who see Greece as a child prodigy who did not live up to its early accomplishments. Rather, we believe that Greece is no instance of Zeno's Achilles paradox and is not bound to fail in its pursuit of national maturity. We believe that this is a nation of great historic achievement and potential and that we are now living through a historic window of opportunity for Greece. But seizing this opportunity will take hard-nosed analysis, introspection, bold vision, and political leadership. This volume is a modest contribution in response to the challenge.

Kalypso Nicolaïdis is Assistant Professor of Public Policy at the John F. Kennedy School of Government, Harvard University.

The author thanks Theodoros Couloumbis, Simon Saunders, and Loukas Tsoukalis for their comments on an earlier version of these remarks.

Greece's assets are well known: its natural and human capital; its geostrategic position at the crossroads of East and West; its partaking in the European Union's (EU) ambitious project for sustained economic prosperity in the region; its people's strong sense of national identity, bolstered by one of the largest, most loyal and most successful diaspora in the world; and, indeed, its historical legacy. Yet, it is all too easy to illustrate how Greece's performance is lacking today. Despite the restoration of democracy two decades ago and the existence of solid democratic institutions, the political system remains ineffective and plagued by clientelism; Greece has repeatedly failed to attract foreign investment and its income per capita has fallen below that of Spain and Portugal; it has come to be viewed—deservedly or not—as the black sheep of Europe. To the outside world, including sympathetic observers from the United States, the most blatant lost opportunity has been Greece's inability to play its natural regional leadership role to help the world cope with the Balkan tragedy. If anything, Greece is perceived as having fanned the flames. Meanwhile, Greeks suppose that the world "simply does not understand" their legitimate fears and goals. But the world would like to understand. The Greek paradox has become other people's business in the post–Cold War era.

Obviously, even for those who share this broad diagnosis, there is room for disagreement on the notion of a paradox. One may argue that the promise has never been that great, nor the performance that bad. After all, as Greeks like to point out, for a nation stymied by four centuries of Ottoman occupation, things are going just fine, especially in comparison with its neighbors. Viewed from another angle, we may recognize that all countries, like all individuals, face some gap between promise and performance. Striving to fill this gap is the engine of progress in history. Or we may simply note that a country is not an input-output table and that comparing intangible potentials with tangible results, counterfactuals with facts, lacks analytical rigor. Ultimately, there is a risk of circular reasoning: if we view the paradox in historical terms, one day's performance is the next day's promise and every effect eventually becomes a cause. We cannot point at once to Greece's structural weaknesses and then to its current inability to fulfill its promise. In the *longue durée*, Greece's status as one of the founders of Western civilization, and the haunting echo of its antique wisdom, may be a curse in disguise. Socrates cannot be held accountable for the nuclear bomb, and modern Greeks cannot be asked to act out a playscript written by their forefathers. We are but one of the many futures of our past. Granted. The Greek paradox is neither a measurable fact nor a museum artifact. It is a metaphor meant to stimulate our thinking, encourage debate and thus—inevitably for Greeks!—spark controversy.

This book should be useful to readers interested not only in Greece per se, but also in the fate of the broader region and in issues of nation building, political and economic development, and foreign policy challenges in the post–Cold War era. Its chapters are drawn from a symposium held at Harvard University's John F. Kennedy School of Government, in fall 1995, whose goal was to contribute to the necessary dialogue among Greeks of all persuasions, as well as between Greeks and non-Greeks, around this most important question: Can Greece take up the challenge? A certain Greek pride, grounded perhaps in an attempt by many in Greece to come to terms with the gap between the promise and the performance, and all too often perceived by others as a superiority complex, often precludes constructive debate between Greeks and non-Greeks on the strengths and weaknesses of the country. This need not be so. Such debates are not only possible but fruitful. If this project makes that much clear, its main objective will have been accomplished.

The book has three sections. In the first section, four prominent political, economic, and security analysts of Greece and its region provide the analytical foundation for better understanding its history, policies, and institutions. Each in their own realm, their contributions assess the causes and consequences of the Greek paradox, focus our attention on factors of change as well as inertia, and provide a basis for prescription. This set of chapters lays the foundation for our jury of commentators. Our goal for the volume is to develop a few concrete proposals and to offer some of our own answers to the perennial question, What is to be done? In section two, key analysts from the United States and Greece remark on the diagnoses offered and add prescriptions of their own. The last section offers "perspectives of policymakers," remarks by three key players who agreed to engage in our dialogue. For students of world politics interested in reciprocal perceptions between "big" and "small" countries, it is fascinating to contrast the views of President Constantine Stephanopoulos with those of former U.S. Assistant Secretary of Defense Joseph Nye, who has since become dean of the Kennedy School. As someone living between the two worlds,

Governor Michael Dukakis offers his moving testimony on what it has meant to be a Greek American as well as an icon for the Greek diaspora. Loukas Tsoukalis, who played a central role in the project, concludes.

In this introduction, I shall summarize the main arguments proposed by the authors and their commentators around the three main themes of politics, economics, and security and conclude by examining the parallel thread weaving through this project: the very real promise held in Greece's relationship with its European partners, the United States, and its worldwide diaspora.

Greek Politics & Society

The political institutions of "the most ancient democracy" in the world can be likened to some foreign words recently introduced into modern Greek language—words that nonetheless turn out to have a Greek etymology. In the last century and a half, through its progressive liberation from the Ottoman Empire and other foreign influences, Greece has imported its institutions—royalty and democracy, for example—in bits and pieces from the West. Through-out this process, and since the time of the Enlightenment, the schism between modernizers and traditionalists, Westerners and Easterners, has been a defining feature of Greek political life—although not unique to Greece. What does the Greek paradox owe to this tension? Have we reached a time when the debate is over, when modernizers and reformists have definitely won?

In his contribution, Nikiforos Diamandouros, a leading academic advocate of modernization, explores the roots of the cleavage between the so-called "reformist" and "underdog" camps and argues that while political reform has been gathering momentum in recent years—and especially with the advent of Mr. Simitis's govern-ment—it is bound to encounter deep forces of resistance that should be anticipated. His version of the Greek paradox contrasts Greece's unprecedented economic performance in the 1950s through the 1970s with its poor performance of the last two decades. Greece achieved full-fledged democratization during the key period from 1974 to 1981, with attendant loss of power by nonaccountable institutions (like the king and the army), the entry of mass parties on the political scene, and the movement of both the Left and the Right toward the center. To explain why Greece "steadily lost ground over the past twenty years," in spite of the normalization achieved in Greek politics, Diamandouros points to the "darker side" of the years of promise, with the buildup of a rather monstrous state bent on the systematic exclusion of all those on the losing side of the civil war, combined with an utterly nonmeritocratic ethos, blatant discrimination in its distribution of social benefits, and harmful overprotection of Greece's fragmented economic system. The structural rigidities and the weakness of Greek civil society, resulting from what the author calls "the logic of particularism," did not prepare the country for the turbulent times ahead.

Despite the watershed victory of the Greek socialist party PASOK in the 1981 elections, the situation perversely worsened. To be sure, PASOK's arrival at the pinnacle of power contributed decisively to the legitimization of Greek democracy through the integration into the system of a whole strata of the population that formerly had been excluded. But this movement only served to intensify the particularist logic of the prior era under the euphemism of "compensatory justice," and to increase the inefficiency and corruption of the state-controlled sector. These developments ran exactly counter to the need for profound structural adjustment called for by Greece's entry into the European Community (EC). For Diamandouros, the prospect of a shrinking state sector and state-dependent private entities, coupled with the gradual adoption of public policies based upon a universalistic logic, is bound to encounter staunch resistance from the existing vested interests that make up the underdog camp. Yet, there have been encouraging gains for reform since the late 1980s in the realm of macroeconomic policy, public management, and relations between business and labor. The election of Constantine Simitis, in January 1996, constitutes the latest and most decisive boost to this process. But, Diamandouros insists, reformists need to focus on minimizing the social and political costs of adjustment if they are to succeed in engineering a metamorphosis of the state "into a flexible instrument of strategic and selective intervention" at the service of Greek society. The author points to a number of concrete approaches to help achieve this goal, from the creation of a more flexible labor market, to the development of continuing education, the independence of the media, and the internal democratization of the parties. We are currently witnessing the awakening of Greek civil society and the mobilization of the social coalition advocating reform and, with this, Diamandouros believes, the promise of a reconstructed, inclusive, and universal Greek citizenship.

Echoing our debates, some may criticize what they see as an externally imposed dichotomy between modernizers and traditionalists. Most contributors to this book, however, make their own variations on this powerful theme. In his comments, Alexis Papahelas echoes the call for radical action against a concentration of power in Greece—particularly in the media—which he sees as a core factor of inertia. Dimitris Keridis notes that the modernization debate is not between those who look to the past and those who look to the future, but between competing views of past and future, and that while the dichotomy is valid, politicians are prone to stress the contrast rather than seek a possible synthesis. To the list of strategies to strengthen the participation of Greek society in the reformist movement, he adds three crucial items: genuine decentralization and local accountability, the buildup of a meritocratic civil service, and the separation of church and state. In his conclusion, Loukas Tsoukalis leaves no ambiguity in his diagnosis of the current situation: the propensity of Greek politics to be defined by populist and charismatic leaders pandering to clienteles has so far survived the era of mass politics in Greece. In short he, too, sees the dualism of modern Greek society as the best explanation of the Greek paradox, but he is not reassuring on the scale of the task ahead. Many in the professional classes, he believes, have been an integral part of this closed system of privilege, and thus have as much an interest as any other group in resisting change. Tsoukalis concludes by delineating even more explicitly the implications of Diamandouros's analysis by suggesting political realignment as a future scenario in Greece, since the political forces favoring reform cut across the two main parties. While such a scenario would clarify the modernization debate in Greece, it also risks polarizing it. The strengthening of the Center Right and Center Left within their respective camps appears more desirable, at least to this day.

The Economic Sphere

Given the thrust of this argument, it is no wonder that the economic sphere is in trouble. Indeed, according to Stavros Thomadakis, the Greek economy remains "chronically backward." This situation sharply contrasts with the individual abilities of Greeks whose success abroad offers ample proof that they are, on the whole, "industrious, adjustable, and capable people." For Thomadakis, however, the gap between ability and performance creates only an apparent paradox—albeit a useful one—since what matters are the intervening variables between the individual and the statistical whole. Thus, his analysis dovetails with that of Diamandouros, both in his assessment of performance and his seeking to draw out the structural variables that affect the Greek economic landscape. Thomadakis presents the economic version of Diamandouros's "darker side" to the "Greek economic miracle"—a period of prosperity that lasted until the mid-1970s, boasting a growth rate almost double the European average. He shows how the trade deficit and unemployment rate during this period indicate deep structural weaknesses in the Greek economy, defects that would only be revealed in the following decades. According to him, this should not surprise us, for Greece labors under handicaps not experienced by other EU countries. In addition to the effects of a protracted period of nation building and devastating wars, Greece is in a bad location: too close to Turkey and too far from Western Europe. Moreover, as both a small and a relatively poor country, it has wavered between the Charybdis of inefficient, small-scale undertakings and the Scylla of oligopolistic heavy industries. This thriving of "large firms in a small market" gives us an additional clue to the politicization of the economy in Greece. Most importantly, Greece is an outward-looking economy, highly vulnerable to international crisis. In 1973, the first oil crisis spelled an abrupt end to the economic miracle and the beginning of a period of low growth and high inflation, which is only recently beginning to subside. Thomadakis provides useful comparative data with Spain and Portugal—the traditional suspects for unflattering contrasts!—showing their much faster recovery after the shock as well as the worrisome lag in Greece's rates of growth of investment and productivity. But there may be some hope in the resilience of Greece's export sector and in the absence of a potentially obsolete industrial base to hinder the country's ability to adjust.

Thomadakis is less critical of the role of the Greek state than Diamandouros. While he concurs in criticizing the use of the regulatory structures as a shield against the crisis in the 1970s, he reckons this was necessary in order to co-opt the Greek electorate into the new democratic game. Tsoukalis, however, makes no compromise with history, bemoaning the fact that "economic adjustment and international competitiveness were sacrificed for many years on the altar of democratic consolidation." What, then, is the potential for economic reform? Thomadakis stresses recent evidence of change in the public sector, while providing his own list of desiderata, including tax reform, mechanisms to coordinate public and private initiatives, political agreement to eliminate the manipulation of taxes for electoral purposes, radical reform of the welfare state, and concurrent privatization and modernization of the public sector. Reform is possible in Greece that combines the harnessing of market forces with a responsible role for a regulatory state. For Thomadakis, the liberalization of the financial sector during the last decade—which he describes in great detail—provides a case in point. The number of other success stories that can inspire the Greeks is growing, as is the consensus that "economic stabilization must precede the satisfaction of social demands." These are signs of collective learning from recent economic history and poor performance, promising signs indeed if such learning eventually leads to an overhaul of Greece's antiquated institutional designs.

Reflecting Thomadakis's diagnosis, the divergence of views between our commentators turns less on goals, more on tactics: use the stick or the carrot? consider the glass half full or half empty? Keridis highlights the pressures for reform that have built up over the years, including those of investors and consumers seeking affordable credit. Tsoukalis puts greater emphasis on the resistance to be expected when structural reforms are implemented, whether from tax evaders responding to the widening of the tax base, from pensioners responding to changes in the social security system, or from workers losing their jobs due to administrative reforms and privatization. Clearly, efforts at stabilization initiated in the early 1990s really started to bite by the mid-1990s, leading to a sharp decrease in the budget deficit and a stronger drachma. These signs of adjustment are to be welcomed. But only if the Greek people can strike a new social contract around radical reform of their state institutions will government be able to move decisively from this new macroeconomic realism to structural economic reform. As Tsoukalis concludes, the challenge will extend well beyond the end of this century.

Greek Foreign & Security Policy

For one, and while there is a broad consensus in Greece that balancing Turkey's military expenditure is a necessary evil, everyone must also agree that the ill-managed relationship with its Aegean neighbor has become an unsustainable drain on Greece's economy. For Greece, perhaps more than for many countries, economics leads to security. The link points to the two greatest challenges facing Greek foreign and security policy in the next five years. For one, everyone agrees that the ill-managed relationship with Turkey has become a drain on Greece's economy. At the same time, if Greece had enough resources to invest in regional economic development, the opportunities awaiting in the Balkans are enormous. How can Greece square this fundamental equation?

Along the same line, Monteagle Stearns, former U.S. ambassador to Greece, takes us back to basics. He argues that, in the field of security, the Greek paradox lies in the gap between military performance and diplomatic potential. Joseph Nye explains that Greece has not exploited its "soft" power to the fullest. And, indeed, one cannot help being puzzled when Greeks testify to their collective sense of insecurity, while at the same time concurring with Nye that Greece constitutes a beacon of stability for countries in the region. To be sure, the challenge here is enormous: Greece's geostrategic situation can be compared to an unwalled city with a coastline to defend three-fourths that of the United States! Thus, says Stearns, "military measures alone cannot defend Greek borders." Only an astute alliance strategy can face up to this challenge, where the fundamental choice for Greece has always been between a land-based alliance to the north and a sea-based alliance to the south. While the purpose of Greece's NATO mission was ostensibly to defend its northern border against communist attack—in coopera-tion with Turkey—every Greek government since the late 1950s has instead concentrated on the perceived threat by Turkey. Stearns cogently points out that, given this focalization on the east, it was the collapse of Yugoslavia, not of the Soviet Union, that created a real challenge to Greek security. Above all, the Macedonian question has plagued Greek diplomacy since the end of the Cold War. And while Stearns absolves Greek passion over the issue as an under-standable product of Greek history, he cannot help but wonder about Greece's incapacity to capitalize on Skopje's dependence, pushing it instead into the arms of competing neighbors. More broadly, and given its outspoken partisanship for the Serbs, Greece has failed to use the Balkan crisis to strengthen its influence in NATO and the European Union. Yet, there is much potential value in these memberships that Greece has left unexploited. In this vein, Stearns praises the new thinking in Greek-Turkish relations exemplified by the lifting of the customs union veto in exchange for promised EU membership for Cyprus. But ultimately, he argues, Greece's future security lies with NATO, given its new Mediterranean outlook and its role as a mechanism to strengthen Greece's precious ties with the United States.

Stearns's sense that Greece has yet to take on the challenges presented by the ending of the Cold War was widely shared in our debates. There were disagreements over just how much better it could have done and what exactly it should do now. "In all, the Greek moment of opportunity has arrived," states Secretary Nye, urging Greece to capitalize on its soft power, including its political and military alliances, in order to play a leadership role in the region. Steve Larrabee sums up the expectations of many in his assessment that "Greece could become the point man of Europe's policy in the Balkans." But the official view from the top in Greece is definitely more cautious, as President Stephanopoulos reminds us that "Greece firmly believes that no Balkan or other neighboring country should involve itself in the ongoing conflict in the Balkans, since this would increase the danger of seeing it spread." This position does leave some room for involvement with soft power—but again, with constraints. Indeed, one can argue that a mediator needs to be either powerful or neutral; Greece is neither. Could it have used or still use its nonneutrality to its advantage? It is not easy for Greece to mediate between Albania and Serbia on Kosovo, while at the same time inquiring about the fate of Greek Albanians in "northern Epirus." How much more could Greece really do? Is its current move toward equidistance designed to lead to higher profile mediation in the region? It should.

Not surprisingly, the Macedonian question is still at the heart of any assessment of how severe the Greek paradox really is. Whatever their own opinion about desirable solutions, Greeks, wherever they live, have shared a frustration during the last few years over the world's lack of understanding of or sympathy for Greece's position. To be sure, the Greek government did receive the benefit of the doubt, as the diplomatic status of the Former Yugoslav Republic of

Macedonia (FYROM) testifies. But most non-Greek as well as some Greek analysts use harsh words to condemn Greek policy *vis-à-vis* FYROM. Greeks unfortunately need to hear Susan Woodward's warning that the Enlightenment view of Greece—which has been its core intangible asset—could erode as "the Greek nationalist hysteria regarding FYROM and persistent Greek preoccupation with Turkey as a hostile threat contribute to an alternative view of Greece." As Stearns sums up, "the Greek embargo isolated Greece politically almost as much as it isolated FYROM economically." Ironically, as Larrabee points out, Greece is the only country in the region that does not have territorial aspirations against Macedonia. This should have led it to engage with, rather than try to isolate, its neighbor. It is not too late to make the connection, and the stakes are high. In his chapter, Misha Glenny issues a passionate plea for defusing the "ethnic time bomb" in Macedonia and urges Greece to build on its recent constructive stance. Echoing the preoccupation of the U.S. administration with Macedonia, Joseph Nye reminds us that Bosnia is only one piece of a complex puzzle in the Balkans, and while he praises Greece's accommodating stance, it seems that more is expected.

Clearly, the Greek government will have much to do in order to address the "credibility deficit"—Larrabee's words—that has resulted from its prior policies. Pulling together the opinions contributed to this book, its strategy should be threefold: to engage in a dialogue over its past policy, to contribute to current reconstruction efforts, and to move to center stage in Western effort to shape the future of the region. On the first front, Greeks need to explain more comprehensively to the world the rationale for their stance on FYROM and ultimately to reappraise their message. In this vein, President Stephanopoulos's address to the Harvard community sought to offer the balanced, official view on the issue, covering the historical landmarks, the ancestral Greek character of the region's population, Bulgaria's ambition to annex the entire region as the cause of the Balkan War and its alliance with Germany to accomplish the task, and, finally, Marshal Tito's "creation" of a Macedonian republic and, by the same token, a Macedonian national identity in Yugoslavia.

Unfortunately, non-Greeks simply do not share the belief deeply held by many Greeks and relayed by the Greek president himself that resistance to the name "Macedonia" is legitimate because such a name is a vehicle for irredentist ambitions. Greeks have a better chance of making themselves heard by stressing the historically shared character of the region, and therefore of Macedonian identity, and by reminding their interlocutors that Greece's tragic civil war was in part fought over Macedonia. Ultimately, Greece will not be taken seriously without acknowledging squarely the legitimate national feelings of two generations of people brought up as "Macedonians." (I have long argued that, for this reason, Greece should have promoted the compromise name of "New Macedonia" from the beginning.) If we accept Papahelas's diagnosis that the foreign policy establishment depends too much on state support to challenge strategic axioms in periods of "overexcitement," then there is some hope for new thinking under the current, more "sober" government.

On the current strategic front, Greece must also take an active part in peace building in Bosnia and, following Glenny, help engineer an overall bargain in the Balkans, linking the south and the north in a regional stability pact. Both Stearns and Larrabee argue for building a Balkan alliance system, while Glenny stresses the key role of the Greek-Bulgarian relationship. Finally, Greece can work at becoming a future political, economic, and cultural hub for the region. It already serves as an engine for the Albanian economy through the remittances of Albanian workers. The Greek president himself has played no small part in building closer economic cooperation with Bulgaria and Romania. These ties need to be encouraged and infrastructures built. For instance, as Thomadakis points out, there will be a need for institutional arrangements to facilitate the security and freedom of payment in the Balkans, which in turn will facilitate trade and economic cooperation. In such a scenario, the city of Thessaloniki has a crucial role to play and needs to develop a coherent strategy to attract the necessary investment.

Ultimately, Greece's sense of security depends on accommodation with its Aegean neighbor. Participants disagreed on whether Greece's interests lay in a strong or a weak Turkey, and therefore when and how it should be engaged. When Joseph Nye urged Greece to take the first, sometimes difficult, steps to build better relationships with its neighbors, he probably had Turkey in mind, along with the Balkans. But Greeks do not see the points on which they can concede. Commenting on the Aegean Sea controversy, President Stephanopoulos makes the case that "the threat by Turkey to declare war against Greece is plainly due to the fact that it is well aware that it lacks any valid argument to support its position." To be sure, Greece was vindicated during the January 1996 crisis over the Imia islets by winning a broad endorsement of its position that the Aegean dispute should be settled by the International Court of Justice at the Hague. Yet, Greeks need to come to terms with the strategic importance of Turkey to the rest of the world and their need, therefore, to make some accommodation in realms other than its territorial integrity. And Greeks need to understand Turkey's concern for a sea route through the Aegean. By distinguishing between process and outcome, a compromise could be found between Greece's insistence on a legal settlement and Turkey's insistence on a political one.

On this premise, several of our commentators argue that Greece can and should engage Turkey in numerous ways. For a start, the Greek strategy to link strategic concessions by Turkey to EU economic benefits can pay off as long as Greece is not seen as reneging on its commitments. Larrabee and others advocate and spell out confidence-building measures between Greece and Turkey. Woodward stresses the need for a regional arms-control regime centered on cooperation between Greece and Turkey, all the more desirable for Greece at a time when Turkey is to be given central responsibility for training the Bosnian army. New ideas need to be generated and initiatives taken along these lines through formal and parallel diplomacy.

The Greek ambassador to the United States, Loucas Tsilas, told the story of a man who encounters an unfriendly group of warriors in the jungle. "Are you with us or with the others?" the warriors ask. "With you," is the man's immediate answer. "Too bad," the warriors' retort, "we are the others." Game theorists may no doubt one day come up with an optimal strategy; in the meantime, Greece must learn to live with the blurring between its own image, reputation, and responsibilities and those of "the other." To be sure, our debates testified to the fact that Greeks, like anyone else, resent being blamed for other people's mistakes—"Others around us are the ones who ignited the fires," "If we live in a bad neighborhood, others, not only us, must police it," or "Others need Greece more than Greece needs others." But at least in geostrategic terms, we do not choose the "other" that we must live with. Negotiation is the name of the game. Tsoukalis describes the pathology of Greek foreign policy as based on a strong sense of insecurity, sometimes culminating in a siege mentality. While it is true that this sense of insecurity is "not created out of nothing," that Greece's neighbors easily turn into enemies, and that Greece's allies have done little to allay Greece's fears, Greek foreign policy, like Greek political life in general, needs to be normalized. Tsoukalis argues that Greek political discourse all too often refers to rights grounded in ancient Greek history. Instead of rights, which are by definition absolute, Greek leaders need to speak more often of Greek interests. This would better prepare Greek public opinion for the give-and-take of international politics and for the political deals that will need to be struck with Skopje and Ankara in the next few years.

Europe, the United States, & the Greek Diaspora

Susan Woodward warns us that isolation is the greatest threat to national survival in a world of interdependence. A last variant of the Greek paradox is that Greece is one of the most open countries in the world, sending out and taking in massive flows of people every year. Yet, the "West" sees Greece as isolating itself in the foreign policy realm, while Greece perceives itself as isolated from the West by a belt of potentially hostile neighbors. In part, there is a gap in perception here regarding the promise versus performance of Greece's alliances. Greece's partners in NATO and the EU stress the enormous comparative advantage this double membership gives Greece in the region; Greeks concur regarding potentials but feel that these alliances do not necessarily deliver. In part, this is due, of course, to the historical baggage of Diamandouros's "institution-alized foreign influence." As Woodward notes, "Greece follows other countries in the region in the conviction that the interests of foreign powers continue to define the realm of the possible." Whatever the mix of perception and reality, Greece and others in the region must be given, and must seek out, the means to shape their own future. Clearly, "Greece needs allies and not patrons"; Stearns's admonition is warranted on both sides. Participants in the debates argued over whether Greece must continue to balance its links to the East and the West or turn definitely to the West. But almost all agree that to use the threat of an Eastern alliance as a lever to obtain satisfaction in the West would be counterproductive. One of Greece's key assets lies in the synergy between three concentric circles of "allies" —Europe, the United States, and the diaspora—whose partnership must be used systematically as a lever to accomplish the transfor-mation goals discussed in this volume.

On how to best use Greece's alliances, certainly a common theme is the need to turn from reactive to proactive strategies. As Basilios Tsingos suggests, going one step further and taking an active role in non-Greek issues that matter to its allies would certainly serve to build a reserve of diplomatic capital. One of the remaining core questions is how to strike the right balance between Europe and the United States, between the European Union, the Western European Union (WEU), and NATO. The tension between Stearns's advocacy of NATO over WEU and Tsoukalis's invocation of the freedom not to choose has been somewhat muted by EU members' decision, led by France, to pursue a NATO-centered European defense identity. A NATO that would commit to addressing disputes between its own members would be especially precious to Greece. It is still the case, however, that how Greece handles its membership in the European Union at the turn of the millennium is the key to its future.

Diamandouros's chapter makes it clear why integration into the European Union in 1981 was not followed by the restructuring of Greek social, political, and economic arrangements that would have been necessary if Greece's developmental trajectory was to converge with that of its new partners. Today, however, Greece is embarking on a difficult agenda of reform and the European Union—more than any individual member state—is an indispensable partner in the reformist coalition. As Tsoukalis argues, membership in the European Union generally acts as a catalyst for reform, even if at the margin the European Union's budgetary transfers can contribute to slowing the need for adjustment. In the last few years, Greece has shown its will to play by the dictates of convergence in the realms of value-added taxes, financial reform, and the criteria for monetary union. Tsoukalis believes that the criteria of convergence for the European Monetary Union (EMU) "will help to concentrate the minds of politicians who may have some difficulty focusing." This is true even if Greece has no illusions of early membership. But Greece also needs to win over its European partners by acting in a constructive manner beyond the mere defense of its own interests, in particular by serving as the guide that many Eastern and Central Europeans believe it to be. Greece also needs to move from the politics of veto to the politics of persuasion and help ensure that the European Union stays focused on managing transitions rather than quasi-permanent exclusions. In doing so, Greece could transfer political capital to other realms, such as back to the European Monetary Union, where it could more credibly take part in the crucial upcoming debate on the fate of the countries at the "periphery"—euphemistically called "pre-ins"—that need to be better heard and represented. It will be a challenging exercise for the Greek government to argue for a flexible and differentiated system while maintaining its growing economic credibility. Maybe not so paradoxically, it is by playing by the rules of the game whenever possible that Greece will be able to advocate changing those rules when really necessary.

If Europe is to be the anchor of Greece's economic and political stability, relations with the United States will remain Greece's insurance policy. In the post–Cold War era, the United States has become the great stabilizer, if only reluctantly and by default. We will never know what our world would have been like if Michael Dukakis had become president of the United States. While, fortunately, the "institutionalized" nature of U.S. influence over Greek politics based on the Truman Doctrine has waned, Greece has yet to become an ally, rather than a client of the United States. There is no doubt that the Greek diaspora in the United States, indeed the Greek lobby in Washington, does count. This may be why Nye feels that the United States is sometimes more sensitive to Greek concerns than the Europeans are. But the U.S.-Greek relationship needs to be nurtured and elevated above the perennial demand for balance with Turkey. For one, it is still the case—and is likely to be for a long time—that U.S. leadership is indispensable in periods of crisis, especially when Turkey is involved. To be sure, the European Union's leverage through accession discussions is not to be discounted. But, in the short run, the U.S. ambassador steps in first. Even in protracted crises, such as the case of Cyprus, U.S. leverage needs to complement the European Union. When Larrabee and others advocate making Cyprus a priority of U.S. diplomacy as a first step in pressuring the Turks and Greeks into normalized relations, he reflects the American preoccupation with the eastern flank, Turkey's stability, and its anchoring to the West. For the United States, Greece is a key piece in a much bigger puzzle that spells balance of power for some and clash of civilizations for others. As far as Greece is concerned, it needs to be reassured that the pieces will be allowed to design their own shape. In this asymmetric relationship between the United States and Greece, perceptions and the changes in dominant paradigms that drive them matter enormously. As Elizabeth Prodromou illustrates, there has been a tendency recently in the United States to consign

Orthodox Greece to one of the "other" civilizational camps. While we certainly need to call for more subtle historical and cultural lenses on the part of U.S. decision makers, Greeks can also refrain from fueling their prejudices. Insisting that the Church stay out of political life, especially foreign policy, would certainly help. Ultimately, Greeks can and should be proud to stand at a crossroads of civilizations—as long as they remain anchored to Western institutions.

To render the Greek paradox more vivid, Thomadakis depicts Greece as poor while "Greeks ... strive the world over as merchants, entrepreneurs, scholars, or engineers." The image is popular, especially among Greeks abroad, but we do not need to assume that there is a Greek gene for genius that is dampened by Greece's waters (he certainly does not!), only that Greek migrants strive like many other nationalities of migrants. What Michael Dukakis's testimony vividly illustrates is the extent to which members of the Greek diaspora are able to combine a deep level of integration and commitment to their new land with strong feelings of attachment to the "homeland." This leads to a sense of solidarity within the diaspora itself that cannot be better captured than by the images of "outpouring support" and "enormous pride" summoned by the former Greek-American presidential candidate. Yet, these feelings of pride and a sense of belonging to some sort of Panhellenic ideal do not, to the same extent as, for instance, the Jewish Diaspora, translate into concrete and continuous ties with the homeland itself. Alexis Papahelas is right in pointing out how too often members of the Greek diaspora's elite who want to lend their expertise, resources, or enthusiasm to specific projects in Greece end up losing interest because the bond has not been nurtured by Greece itself. A new definition of "associate citizenship" is needed for Greeks abroad that can fulfill their frequent yearning to "contribute" without allowing them to pretend to know best "what is good for Greece."

The Greek diaspora, not only in the United States but also around the world, unquestionably has a role to play in fostering change in Greece. It can help create spaces for constructive and bipartisan dialogue by supporting initiatives such as an independent foundation for the future of Hellenism, as called for by Papahelas, or the already existing network of the Hellenic Resource Institute, launched by Greek students in the United States. Greek immigrants can also continue playing an advocacy role for Greece in the realm of foreign policy by explaining its fears, hopes, and dilemmas in their own words. Greece must be told through their personal odyssey rather than that of Alexander the Great. But, as Dukakis pleads, this advocacy role requires a clear message emanating from Greece itself. Conversely, members of the diaspora can bring their experience in their adopted country to bear by contributing to debates in Greece over democratization, economic reform, or the information revolution. Often seen themselves as minorities in their adopted countries, members of the Greek diaspora could even contribute by raising the ultimate taboo subject in Greece, namely the status of minorities. Clearly, members of the diaspora do not, by definition, play only a constructive role, and we must not underestimate the risk, stressed by Woodward, that while their beliefs were formed in a previous period, they have enormous autonomy in defining the perceived interests of their homeland. This is all the more reason why the contribution of the diaspora must be conceived of as an ongoing interaction rather than as two unilateral streams of propaganda from the homeland and support from abroad.

What Is to Be Done?

In each of the areas discussed in this book, as one of our commentators declares, "the time for reformist thinking has arrived." The contributors provide a range of concrete policy proposals, some controversial, others less so, that we hope will serve the current and lively debate over Greece's future. They discuss extensively options for political, economic, and institutional reform that could form the basis for a new national debate. Tsingos sums up the challenge as a need for policymakers to lengthen the shadow of the future for all actors in Greece. But, ultimately, what needs to be questioned in Greece is as much the state of mind as the state of things. Participants in this project call for a shift from an attitude of entitlement to a spirit of participation, from a focus on Greek rights to an articulation of Greek interests, and from a defensive posture to a proactive approach to its relations with neighbors and allies. Most generally, and to paraphrase Woodward, there is a post–Cold War paradox in the contrast between the proclaimed hope of tearing down territorial and ideological curtains and the ubiquitous resurgence of policies and philosophies of exclusion. Greece can address this paradox by designing its own policies of inclusion, domestically, in the region, and with Greeks around the world. We do not claim to have found ways to resolve the "Greek paradox," or even to have presented a consensus on what this paradox really is about. We do, however, believe, unlike Zeno, that Achilles can catch up to the Tortoise and that Greeks are committed to the promise.

Assessing the
"Greek Paradox"

Chapter 2

P. Nikiforos
Diamandouros

Greek Politics &
Society in the 1990s

The paradox of modern Greece—its potential in contrast to its actual achievement—is indeed real. Judged by a number of indicators, Greek performance in the past two decades has lagged relative to the promise suggested by its achievements in the previous two decades. To understand why and to be able to propose potential remedies to the situation, we need to grasp the complex logics underlying the period of promise (roughly, 1950 to the 1970s) and the period of disappointment (mid-1970s to the present), and the intimate relationship between the two.

From Civil War to Great Expectations:
The Context of Promise (1950s–70s)

The immediate post–civil war years (1950–70) were, without a doubt, a period of unprecedented socioeconomic change in Greece. Driven forward by a 6.6 percent average rate of growth, exceeded, throughout this period, only by that of Japan and, occasionally, Israel, Greece was literally transformed from an underdeveloped economy and society into a very promising, newly industrializing country. Major manifestations of this profound transformation were (a) a highly successful rural electrification program; (b) the rebuilding of an infrastructure destroyed almost completely by ten years of foreign occupation, civil strife, and outright civil war during the 1940s; (c) high rates of urbanization; (d) significant increases in literacy; (e) a clear rise in industrial production and, more generally,

P. Nikiforos Diamandouros is Professor of Political Science at the University of Athens. He serves as Director-Chairman of the National Centre for Social Research (EKKE), and President of the Greek Political Science Association.

(f) the gradual but unmistakable ascendancy in Greek society of cultural practices and values intimately linked with modernity. What made all this change all the more remarkable was that it was, for the most part, achieved without the social pathologies so closely associated with shantytowns in Latin America and bidonvilles in North Africa and elsewhere in the developing world.

By the 1970s, therefore, Greece, along with a handful of other newcomers, appeared to be well on its way to claiming its position in the charmed circle of the so-called First World. In many ways, this goal was attained in the critical seven-year period between 1974, when Greece established its first-ever, fully democratic political system, and 1981, when it entered the European Community. The democratization of Greek politics can be regarded as an extension into the realm of politics of the deeply transformative process of modernization, which, in the previous decades, had already profoundly changed the dynamics of Greek society and its economy. The democratization of the Greek political system entailed both negative and positive dimensions. Negatively, it signaled the elimination from the Greek political center stage of nondemocratically accountable political structures, such as the monarchy, the armed forces, and institutionalized foreign influence (after 1947, the United States). In the context of the anticommunist logic that dominated the post–civil war years (1950–74), these structures had been accorded *de facto* and *de jure* veto powers over crucial policy areas ("reserved domains") that systematically subverted the democratic process.[1]

---

1. The Greek monarchy, an institution with a long and controversial history of direct involvement in politics and intimately identified with the excesses of the anticommunist state of the post–civil war period, was abolished, in December 1974, by a plebiscite held under conditions universally acknowledged to be fair and free of coercion.

Sobered by their experience at direct rule and chastised by their misguided involvement in, and failure to cope effectively with, the disastrous Cyprus crisis and subsequent Turkish invasion of that state, the Greek armed forces withdrew to the barracks and, for the first time in six decades, accepted the principle of civilian control of the military.

The institutionalized nature of foreign influence in Greek politics and society dates to the birth of modern Greece in the nineteenth century and to the conditional sovereignty enjoyed by the Greek state for more than a century and a half. By far the most powerful of these influences were the British, which lasted until 1947, and the American, which began with the proclamation of the Truman Doctrine and came to an end in the 1970s.

The democratization of Greek politics involved four distinct components: first, the elevation of democratically accountable institutions, such as parliament and the governments issuing from it, to positions of political preeminence typical of fully democratic political systems; second, the significant expansion of "political space" and the occupation of the heretofore "off-limits" Center-Left area by PASOK, a noncommunist party of the Left; third, the modernization of the Greek Right. Recognizing the challenge to its preeminence symbolized by the birth of PASOK and by the democratization of the political system, the Right *(a)* abandoned its identification with fanatical anticommunism and its weak commitment to fully democratic politics, and *(b)* rallied around a new, moderate, Center-Right political formation, appropriately named New Democracy. Fourth, the emergence, for the first time in Greek history, of mass political parties capable of effectively organizing and mobilizing their adherents in support of or against particular policies or goals. Taken together, these changes signaled the normalization of Greek politics and, after more than half a century of failed attempts, its convergence with modern, democratic political systems elsewhere.

From Great Expectations to Stagnation: The Context of Disappointing Performance (1980s–present)

Under these circumstances, Greece's entry into the European Community in 1981 could legitimately be regarded as the crowning achievement of a longer-term process of socioeconomic and political modernization. Such modernization rendered the country eligible for membership in the ranks of advanced industrial societies and opened new opportunities for further advances and for a deeper integration into their midst.

To understand why this did not happen and why, instead of advancing, Greece has steadily lost ground over the past twenty years, one has to look to the darker side of the success story told so far. There were three structural weaknesses in that success story, whose negative influence is still with us today. First and foremost was the strategy of governance of the anticommunist state in post–civil war Greece, which hinged on the maintenance of a discriminatory and, in the final analysis, vindictive political system that deliberately distinguished between victors and vanquished in the civil war. Measured in terms of concrete policy outcomes, this strategy translated into a systematic exclusion from the ever-expanding state and public sector of all those who, because of actual or alleged involvement with the losing side in the civil war, were unable to obtain from state security agencies a certificate testifying to their "healthy," that is, anticommunist, political views and constituting a necessary prior condition for employment in state-controlled sectors.

A direct by-product of the use of explicitly political, nonmerito-cratic, and clientelistic criteria for state employment was that the Greek civil service and state-controlled enterprises were staffed with personnel often deficient in necessary skills but possessed of powerful political connections, rendering them quasi-immune to effective quality control and prone to corruption.

In addition, given the incapacity of the Greek economy, despite its successes, to absorb the surplus labor left behind by a major emigration wave to Western Europe, the state-controlled sector emerged as the largest employer in the country, at the obvious cost of enormous overstaffing that rendered it all the more inefficient. Finally, a state sector so constituted was decidedly partisan in orientation and clearly at odds, for reasons of political ideology, with significant segments of society.

The second structural weakness arose from the manner in which state policies affecting large groups in society were conceived of and applied during the period of growth. The distinguishing feature of these policies was their underlying *particularistic* logic that guided the distribution of social and economic benefits in society. The major advantage of such a modus operandi was the great flexibility that it afforded the state in responding to demands from diverse groups and in implementing policies for the allocation of benefits to them. But the absence of *universalistic* criteria governing the process of benefit allocation effectively translated into fewer constraints placed upon the state, thereby increasing its indepen-dence *vis-à-vis* society.

The price paid for that system was enormous in the long run. To begin with, it contributed to the gradual construction of a social and economic policy landscape characterized by immense variation, fragmentation, and division. Over time, it resulted in the systematic breakup of social forces, on both the capital and the labor side. In turn, such a policy outcome *(a)* exacerbated the fragility of a Greek civil society already greatly weakened by the traumatic experiences of foreign occupation and civil war; *(b)* placed effective barriers to its capacity to hold the state accountable for its actions; *(c)* effectively prevented the emergence of new solidaristic arrangements to legitimize the state; and *(d)* produced widespread perceptions of inequity that greatly undermined the legitimacy of the postwar system and the market mechanism identified with it. These dysfunctional aspects of postwar state-society relations became particularly noticeable during the period of the colonels' authoritarian regime (1967–74) and were to extend into the post-authoritarian period with especially harmful consequences.

The third structural weakness of Greece's postwar success story grew directly out of the second and served as the other side of the same coin. This was so because, to the extent that the particularistic (and clientelistic) logic of the state's operation contributed heavily to the enormous fragmentation of productive structures, it also rendered the state's protective umbrella all the more necessary for their continued growth and survival. Seen in this light, the country's postwar "miracle" can be said to have been intimately linked with the emergence a ubiquitous, overinterventionist, overregulating, paternalistic, and protectionist state.

The best illustration of the situation was the development of an enormous self-employed sector, arguably the largest in the European Community/Union, absorbing, at present, over forty percent of the Greek labor force. This sector of the labor market was dominated by extremely small and often noncompetitive productive structures, dependent on state regulation and protection for survival, thriving on illicit or illegal practices and links with the state apparatus, extremely prone to tax evasion, and imparting a protean quality to Greek economic culture that has adversely affected the quality of its political life and institutions.

Put otherwise, the combined outcome of fragmentation, overprotection, overregulation, and political penetration was the emergence of a social, economic, and political environment characterized by pronounced structural rigidities which exacerbated the weakness of Greek civil society. Such an environment effectively undermined *(a)* society's potential for autonomous organization; *(b)* its capacity to address some of these problems through the political process and the central institutions of the state; and *(c)* its ability to adjust to the rigors of greatly changed circumstances in the 1970s and beyond.

The first unmistakable signs of a dwindling Greek miracle came in the late 1960s. Though obscured by the euphoria that seized the country at the end of the colonels' authoritarian rule and, especially, by the establishment and consolidation of democracy in the 1970s and early 1980s, Greece's model of socioeconomic development, based on the central role which the logic of particularism had assigned to the state in the productive process and in the regulation of economy and society, had reached its insuperable limits.

Seen in this light, 1981 acquires distinction as a watershed year in which Greece was drawn into two qualitatively different processes of *integration*, one domestic and one international, that had far-reaching and contradictory impacts on the evolution of its politics and society. The *domestic* process, set off by PASOK's major electoral victory in that same year, entailed the integration into Greece's new democratic system of the large social strata previously excluded and/or marginalized by the anticommunist state in the postwar years. The significance of that process cannot be overemphasized. Its failure could well have undermined the legitimacy of the new democratic order in the eyes of millions of Greeks and jeopardized its very viability. Its success, primarily manifested through *(a)* extensive renewal of personnel, reaching, in many ways, from the top to the bottom of Greek society; and *(b)* a redistribution of income and social benefits in favor of newly empowered groups, greatly contributed to the deepening of the new system's roots and to the legitimation of Greek democracy.

The deeper cost of this success, however, was high and long-lasting, for two major reasons. First, the redistribution of social benefits was carried out in an overtly particularist fashion that not only replicated the practices of the past, but also enlarged their scope and intensity. Second, the particularistic logic informing the redistribution of social and economic benefits ran directly counter to the universalistic logic of democratization underpinning the political empowerment of heretofore marginalized and/or excluded social strata.

Employing the distinctly populist logic of "compensatory justice," subsequently invoked by its conservative rival, New Democracy, PASOK inaugurated a new practice in Greek politics. The newly discovered power of the mass party organization was systematically, inventively, and ruthlessly employed to secure "tangible compensation," in the form of employment or privileged access to resources, for partisan supporters having suffered inequities, real or perceived, under previous administrations or regimes.

Irrespective of which side applied it, the results of this practice were decidedly adverse and pervasive. The state-controlled sector experienced yet another increase and was staffed, once again, by individuals possessing low skills and selected using nonmeritocratic criteria and clientelistic logics geared to the satisfaction of particularistic demands. The prevalence of such practices in the state-controlled sector and the values, mentalities, and behaviors associated with them produced two negative spill-over effects. First, it contributed to the emergence in the private sector of noncompetitive, state-dependent enterprises run according to the same logic and principles. Second, it brought forward a new political class characterized, for the most part, by lack of leadership skills and vision, fear of responsibility, obsession with narrowly constructed "political costs," mediocrity, and proneness to corruption. More generally, it spawned an overall cultural climate inclined towards introvertedness, the defense of vested interests, and the absence of strategic thinking, at the very time when Greece's entry into the European Community made imperative a move in the exact opposite direction.

In short, the domestic process of integration just described contributed to the consolidation of Greek democracy at the cost of (a) greatly adding to the inefficiency and corruption of the state-controlled sector; (b) expanding the "social space" occupied by state-dependent and mostly noncompetitive enterprises in the private sector; (c) further weakening civil society's capacity to pursue reform successfully ; (d) eroding the legitimacy of new political elites whose rise to power reflected the problems of the logic of particularism; and (e) significantly debasing the quality of democracy and the legitimacy of the state in that country.

The *international* integration process into which Greece found itself deeply drawn in the 1980s has to be understood on two levels. On the one hand, the country's entry into the European Community signaled its incorporation into a transnational, European process, whose logic necessitated not merely the further modernization but also the restructuring of Greek social, political, and economic structures, if the country's developmental trajectory was to converge with that of its new partners. On the other, Greece's membership in the European Community and its deeper integration into the international economic system exposed it much more directly to the dislocations caused by the oil crises of the 1970s and to the pressing need for structural readjustments.

Thus, at the very moment when the international and European environments were entering a period (1980s and 1990s) that was to be increasingly dominated by demands for the streamlining and rationalization of state structures, by persistent calls for deregulation and privatization, and by the search for developmental strategies supporting competitiveness, capital intensive forms of production based on highly skilled labor forces, and the capacity for flexible adaptation to the rapidly changing conditions of the international markets, Greece found itself the hostage of social and political forces pushing it in the opposite direction.

This analysis suggests three premises for thinking about future reform. First, that Greece's inability consistently to pursue reform strategies necessary for its further integration into the advanced industrial world is due, above all, to the enormous staying power of its large, noncompetitive social strata, whose recently secured positions of power and privilege are mortally threatened by the prospects of structural reform. Second, that, despite powerful opposition, the forces favoring reform and identifying with alternative, universalistic logics of social change are gradually gaining momentum. And third, that reform should be regarded as a one-way policy option, the reversal of which would have extremely adverse implications for Greece's future. Let me elaborate.

The fundamental transformation of the European and international environments in the last two decades have laid bare the structural weaknesses of Greece's model of socioeconomic transformation. The tenacious opposition to reform in Greece stems primarily from two intimately linked forces: the state-controlled sector and the self-employed sector. The state-controlled sector encompasses the civil service and the powerful public utilities that enjoy monopolistic or oligopolistic status in the economy. These entities include the Public Power Corporation (ΔEH), the Greek Telecommunications Organization (OTE), the major shipyards, Olympic Airways, and, to a lesser extent, the banking sector, close to ninety percent of which is still under direct or indirect state control. The extraordinarily large self-employed sector amounts to roughly forty percent of the Greek labor force and is mostly characterized by small, if not tiny, labor-intensive practices, low skills, and low capitalization. For reasons already described, these

small enterprises and the social forces associated with t/
resist any change of circumstances that would deprive
state protection that has allowed them to live comfortably or, more
recently, to survive precariously. It is the prospect of *(a)* the
shrinking of the state sector and the noncompetitive, state-dependent, or self-employed entities in the private sector; and *(b)* the
gradual adoption of public policies encouraging universalistic over
particularistic logics, that leads social forces associated with them
to oppose reform measures, however moderate, designed to free
state and market in Greece from built-in rigidities geared to the
perpetuation of antiquated structures and practices and to the
defense of vested interests. The social and political weight of these
forces and the political clout that they can collectively marshal in
opposition to change has produced a reinforcing cleavage cutting
through Greek society and its major institutions, creating two
sharply opposing camps, which I have elsewhere labeled as
reformist and underdog.[2]

Despite it all, the signs that reformist forces are making headway
in Greece are proliferating. The single most important factor
pointing in that direction is the growing awareness of both elites
and the public at large that the Greek economy is in dire need of
reform along lines that eschew the failed experiments of the past.
Despite the worrying persistence of some voices, a policy of
economic austerity, inaugurated in 1985–87, has been pursued by
all administrations, irrespective of which party was in power, since
the early 1990s. The positive cumulative results of these policies are
apparent at many levels: important indicators of economic performance, such as the rate of inflation, interest rates, state tax
revenues, and economic growth have been consistently moving in
the right direction. The banking system has undergone major
reform in the past ten years and more change seems to be inevitable. The anemic Athens stock market is being overhauled, and draft
legislation designed to render it responsive to the opportunities of
the evolving international economic environment is in its final

---

2. See P. Nikiforos Diamandouros, *Cultural Dualism and Political Change in Post-
Authoritarian Greece* (Madrid: Centro Juan March de Estudios Avanzados en Ciencias
Sociales, 1994, Estudio 50). The conflict between these two camps became glaringly
obvious in the intense intraparty tensions which broke out in PASOK, once physical
incapacity forced Andreas Papandreou to retire from active politics and Constantine
Simitis, a man long identified with reformist goals, became prime minister.

stages of preparation. Measures are currently being taken to ensure freedom from the stifling provisions of the antiquated public accounting system and to promote the adoption of flexible methods of responding to opportunities created by the domestic and international economic environment. The recent announcement concerning the creation of special monitoring units (MOΔ) to observe the operation of public enterprises is a case in point. Lastly, the dual attempt by the Ministry of Finance both to expand the tax base and to enforce existing tax legislation in such a way as to capture a wide array of tax-evading groups, located mostly in the protean self-employed sector, has spawned a climate of improved social equity that has translated into an improvement of the state's perennially weak legitimacy.

At the level of institutions and social forces, the rapprochement which, in the past few years, has taken place between the Federation of Greek Industries (SEB) and the Confederation of Greek Workers (GSEE), the resulting change in the patterns of collective bargaining, the longer duration of collective agreements, the establishment of a research institute by GSEE, the activation of the National Labor Institute—a venture jointly sponsored by SEB and GSEE—and, above all, the growing independence of the trade unions from stifling state control, which was the rule until the late 1980s, constitute tangible gains in the overall trend favoring reform. It is worth noting that this trend is reflected in the recent annual reports of various international organizations (e.g., OECD, IMF, EU). The election, in January 1996, of Constantine Simitis as the new prime minister of Greece is widely expected to enlarge the prospects of the reformist camp, in which the new premier has played a leading role.

Still, all positive signs notwithstanding, the situation continues to be fragile and, in a number of ways, precarious. The major resistance to structural change is located precisely where the stakes are highest: in the state-controlled sector, where the much-needed process of deregulation and privatization has proceeded at an agonizingly slow pace. The fiercest opposition to change has been in the area of privatization, precisely because it involves shrinking the labor force employed by the state sector and, hence, threatens powerful entrenched interests.

In the self-employed sector, the various associations representing the interests of its heterogeneous constituencies are engaging in defensive mobilization strategies. Their goal is to contain the threats posed by a new and fast-changing market environment increasingly dominated by large, modern, and well-capitalized enterprises owned by big chains often in partnership with foreign firms. This conflict is especially visible in the production and distribution of foods and beverages, the garment industry, and more generally, the retail sector. And the trend is unmistakably unfavorable for the social coalition of forces opposing change.

Challenges for the Future

The opportunities emerging from the preceding analysis are pretty clear: the *objective* environment in which Greece is operating as a result of its entry into the European Union (and, through it, into an increasingly global economy) makes structural reform a nonreversible policy option for the country. (In current circumstances, "going it alone" is hardly an option, even for large and powerful states.) The big problem, then, is two-pronged: first, how to bring about the *subjective* awareness that the option is unavoidable to help legitimate the process of change and render it more acceptable to the large social strata affected by it; and second, how to devise policies that minimize the high social and political costs of structural change. I shall organize my answers around six major areas: the state-controlled sector, the self-employed sector, education, the mass media, the political parties, and civil society. But first, a general point.

The fundamental prerequisite for furthering reform in Greece is to broaden and strengthen the social coalition espousing it and to help tip the balance of forces in its favor. The distinguishing features of that coalition are two: first, it is qualitatively strong, because of (a) its powerful appeal among the more modern, competitive, and dynamic sectors and social strata in Greek society; (b) the political support, whether direct or diffuse, it receives from the European Union; and (c) the increased legitimacy of using universalistic logics in formulating public policy. Second, the coalition is numerically weak, because of its limited appeal among the large social strata threatened by the prospect of reform.

Given this balance of forces, it is imperative that the implementation of necessary reforms be accompanied by policies designed to blunt the inevitably high human costs associated with restructuring. To do otherwise would risk the possibility of a major reaction among the large social strata affected by reform, which, in extremis, could be politically destabilizing. This is especially the case, given the potential for xenophobic reaction to the major role being played by the European Union as a partner in the reformist coalition. In practical terms, this means that the reform options available to Greece should steer clear of neoliberal formulae of Thatcherite provenance. They should instead rely on a qualitative transformation of the role of the state in Greece, a development that will entail its withdrawal from direct involvement in production and excessive regulation of economic and social arrangements. This metamorphosis should render the state a flexible instrument of strategic and selective intervention designed to encourage the formulation of public policy based on universalistic logics, to enhance the competitiveness of Greek social and economic structures, to promote the empowerment of civil society, and to improve the quality of state-society relations and, ultimately, of democracy in that country.

The State-controlled Sector

However meekly, reforms in this area have already begun to move in the right direction, albeit more in the realm of deregulation than in the more intractable area of privatization. What is needed, at this stage, is the adoption of clear and unequivocal policies concerning both deregulation and privatization and their consistent implementation in a manner that enhances the state's credibility and legitimacy. The goal should be to bring about, first, a major reduction in size of the civil bureaucracy and the wider public sector. This can be achieved by providing incentives for early retirement, so structured as to appeal to the less skilled rather than the more skilled workers. Second, sharp curtailment of new entrants coupled with *(a)* a major upgrading of the requirements for entry and *(b)* their meritocratic application. In addition, the reform agenda should include the adoption of major retraining and skill-building programs, including, in particular, the introduction of automation, information technology, and modern management techniques to run the civil service and, especially, the powerful public utilities, banks, and corporations.

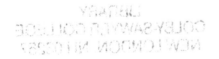

The Self-employed Sector

To mitigate the inevitable pain associated with the Greek version of "death of a salesman," three policy packages seem to be needed: first, the creation of the legal and financial environment to promote the merger of Greece's "nanoenterprises" into larger, more competitive and viable units. Here, properly targeted, nonwasteful use of European Union funds for small and medium-sized enterprises can play a crucial role, politically legitimating the adjustment process.

The second policy needed provides multiple "exit routes" out of self-employment, designed to facilitate the reintegration of those who choose not to consolidate their enterprises. Here, two large trends seem to be emerging: first, the increasing attraction of franchising arrangements, whose fast growth suggests the capacity to absorb a large part of the labor force that is leaving self-employment, while, at the same time, exposing workers to new and decidedly modern daily practices and routines that contribute to the adoption of modern attitudes, values, and behavior. Second, a similar movement in the direction of subcontracting is also growing.

Last, a policy package is needed that provides for greatly expanded retraining and skill-building services capable of channeling part of the labor force released from self-employment into a productive, wage-earning labor market. New flexible arrangements are needed that allow part-time employment and the use of information technologies to work from one's home to accommodate the needs of the new, specialized labor market.

Education

This subject is much too large to examine in any detail here. Nevertheless, success in the implementation of the type of arrangements described above hinges on at least four developments in education: (a) the overhaul of normal schools to produce teachers practicing modern teaching methods that emphasize critical thinking over rote learning and memorization as well as the use of information technologies; (b) an expansion of the range of post-secondary institutions designed to respond to the ever-growing career opportunities, specializations, and options generated by the information age; (c) legislative provision for continuing education in both the state and the private sectors, with an eye to creating a more competitive labor force and to contributing to the emergence of a more modern economic culture capable of furthering Greece's integration into the modern world; and (d) structural reform in the country's university system (curriculum, research, entrance requirements for students, hiring and promotion requirements for staff) and the lifting of the constitutional prohibition on private institutions of higher learning.

Mass Media

Despite their youth, the Greek mass media are widely perceived as playing too pervasive and negative a role in the country's politics. Without a doubt, we are witnessing, in this field as well, a fierce battle for survival through consolidation, at the end of which (that is, in the next few years), a small number of large structures combining television, radio, and newspapers will share this highly lucrative market.

Recent legislation in this area leaves a great deal to be desired and attests to the state's preference for continued fragmentation that maximizes its freedom of movement *vis-à-vis* the industry. What is urgently needed are measures designed *(a)* formally to remove the state from direct involvement in this field; *(b)* to strengthen the powers of an independent public authority (already in place) to regulate the industry and to exercise some restraining influence on its direct links with political structures; and, more generally; *(c)* to adopt clear, rational, and transparent rules and procedures concerning the operation of the mass media and their relationship with the state that contribute to a stable and predictable environment governing the operation of this important sector. I hasten to add that the success or failure of such an undertaking will, in the final analysis, hinge on its capacity to regulate (and, if need be, sever) the often intimate links currently existing among political parties, mass media, and major public procurement projects that form the basis for widespread allegations of illicit if not illegal transactions involving the three.

Political Parties

The major reform here should be the democratization of the parties. Having successfully transformed themselves from parties of notables into mass parties with powerful central organizations, Greek political parties now need to move to the next stage in their historical development and institute mechanisms promoting internal democracy, which will undoubtedly have a powerful spillover effect on society as a whole. Movement in that direction by one party will more than likely generate a transformative dynamic that will cause the others to follow, for reasons of survival. The result will be beneficial all around.

Civil Society
The cumulative effect of substantive reform in the areas outlined above will be the empowerment of Greek civil society to change its traditional patterns of interaction with the state. The adoption of universalistic logics in the formation of public policies can help generate new and more durable solidaristic arrangements within society. These arrangements can, in turn, enhance the legitimacy of the state and contribute to the gradual erosion of the culture of cynicism and distrust in state-society relations that is the major long-term legacy of particularism in modern Greece.

By emphasizing mechanisms that promote the construction of social coalitions along more egalitarian lines, such a change can greatly contribute to the further democratization of Greek society and significantly enhance the quality and durability of Greek democracy. Finally, changes in this direction will set in motion a longer-term process, whose final outcome could well be the emergence of an alternative collective, modern Greek identity based more on the universalistic and inclusive principle of citizenship than on the exclusive and particularistic criterion of ethnicity. Such an eventuality will help anchor Greece more firmly in the modern world.

The recent proliferation of "citizens' movements" in the country, the growing assertiveness in certain judicial quarters in defense of environmental rights, and the formation of the new government headed by Constantine Simitis could be signs that the social coalition actively advocating reform is expanding its scope, acquiring a new dynamic, and reaching out to new potential allies. It is this much-needed broadening which, despite continuing challenges from quarters engaging in concerted rearguard action designed to stall change, will, in the final analysis, enable the reform coalition to tip the balance of forces within Greece in its favor and translate what, at present, is a precarious advantage into permanent ascendancy. The Greek diaspora and the reform-oriented forces in Europe and North America can play an important role in making this goal a reality and, in the process, helping resolve the "Greek paradox."

Chapter 3

*Stavros B.
Thomadakis*

The Greek Economy:
Performance,
Expectations, &
Paradoxes

A fundamental paradox exists in the Greek economy: Greeks are industrious, adjustable, and capable people, who thrive the world over as merchants, entrepreneurs, scholars, engineers, yet the Greek economy is not performing well. It remains chronically backward in comparison to the economies of other European countries and has fallen behind even the economies of southern European countries such as Spain and Portugal. Greece has received very little of that important economic vote of confidence called private foreign investment compared with the rest of Europe. Its external accounts have remained afloat largely due to large public transfers from the European Union (EU), support which cannot be maintained forever. Is there a real paradox, or can this discrepancy between ability and performance be explained? And, if a paradox exists, what does it take for the discrepancy to be corrected and for Greece to be set upon a path of new economic growth?

The paradox between ability and performance is only an apparent one. Individual abilities do not automatically translate into collective performance. Intervening factors play a role in the transformation of abilities into results and in the aggregation of results into collective performance. It is the search for, and the understanding of, these factors that hold the answer to the seeming paradox of Greek economic performance.

Contrasts and seeming paradoxes have often informed Greek public debates on the economy in a useful way. At least two come to mind. In the last few years, and in the context of widespread tax

Stavros B. Thomadakis is Professor of Financial Economics at the University of Athens.

evasion and public deficits, one frequently hears that Greek citizens are rich whereas the Greek state is poor. Although not accurate—not all Greeks are rich and not only rich Greeks evade taxes—the seeming paradox underpins ideologically the efforts to bring about serious tax reform. One is also reminded of the famous remark by Prime Minister George Papandreou, who said, thirty years ago, that "in Greece numbers thrive but people suffer." Spoken at a time of rapid economic growth, the phrase addressed the need for better distribution of the benefits of the new prosperity. Again, the contrast underpinned ideologically the goal of social and economic reform, reform that might have saved the Greek economy from many dislocations later on had it been achieved at that time. Paradoxes, even if only apparent, play a role in creating a focus on desired political change. The paradox of ability versus performance is a useful one in this respect, as it serves to focus Greek energies on what can be achieved and how to achieve it.

Any discussion of the Greek economy must of course be based on indices of performance. The choice of indices, the choice of time periods for measurement, and the choice of benchmarks for comparison are all important issues. Minimal protection against bias will be provided in this paper by three means. First, performance will be measured with adequate time depth, so that the starting period of observation will not matter so much. This means providing both a brief qualitative review of long-term historical performance and time-averaged indices of performance over recent periods. Second, performance will be measured by few but wide-ranging indices that capture as many aspects of the economy as possible. Third, simple comparison with other European Union member countries, and separately with Portugal and Spain, will afford an assessment of Greek performance in the European context.

In the search for proposals for changes and solutions, it is always desirable to be taught by experience gained from successful reforms. In that respect, the Greek financial sector will be used as an example of successful reform and positive change already occurring in the economy.

The paper is presented in four sections: (1) a brief overview of historical economic performance of Greece; (2) a presentation of indices of recent performance and comparative assessments; (3) a discussion of the Greek financial sector as a paradigm of successful reform; and (4) conclusions.

A Historical Perspective

In the 167 years of independent statehood, periods of economic growth in Greece have been few and far between. In the nineteenth century, episodes of growth were seen in the 1850s and the 1880s. In the twentieth century, equally sparse growth was recorded in the 1920s, and again in the 1960s. For the greater part of its history, modern Greece has been in a state of economic stagnation, even crisis. This is not hard to explain. In the nineteenth century, the country was burdened by large debts (contracted during the revolutionary period of the 1820s) and by an irredentist mission that held it almost continuously at the brink of war and kept its frontiers unsettled. In the twentieth century, when Greece had acquired its current frontiers, it suffered, in addition to the two world wars that engulfed all of Europe, the Balkan wars in the 1910s, the Asia Minor war with its ensuing mass immigration in the 1920s, and the civil war in the 1940s. Even during the intervals of peace, Greece had to overcome towering obstacles in order to fuel a growth process, obstacles rooted both in geography and in history.

Greece's small size, in my estimation, has been a perennial disadvantage for industrial development; the combination of a small population and low incomes has made its internal market too small, as measured by industrial standards of minimum efficient size, which have been growing consistently throughout the century. Countries like Greece that have started out with both small-scale and low incomes normally require an exceptional combination of factors to break out of these restrictions in a competitive world. Successful export development appears necessary. For industrial latecomers, however, manufacturing exports are much harder to achieve on a sufficient scale than nonindustrial ones, and Greece has not escaped this basic rule. For many decades, the list of its major export items consisted of agricultural products and services. On the manufacturing front, the small domestic market supported light industry but discouraged "intermediate" or "heavy" industry.

Thus, Greek disadvantages in several heavy or intermediate industrial sectors, where economic production requires large-scale undertakings, have consistently skewed actual investment in industry toward light manufacturing, labor-intensive activities, and small-firm organizations. Indeed, most Greek manufacturing to this day can be found in sectors and activities that neither require the costs nor gain the benefits of large-scale production and marketing. In 1988, food, beverage, textile, and clothing manufacturing represented over 40 percent of total manufacturing employment in the country. Furthermore, in the same year, 99 percent of manufacturing establishments and 64 percent of manufacturing employment were organized in enterprises employing less than fifty persons.[1]

In the few cases where Greek manufacturing undertakings have ventured into heavy industry, the logic of large scale has led to the creation of oligopolies, for example, in the metallurgy, shipbuilding, and cement sectors. The expected impact of oligopolies on an economy is magnified in Greece. Besides the classic problems of higher prices and relative slowness of innovation, their large size relative to the whole economy consistently leads to their entanglement in the business of the state and politics. Over the last thirty years, the disposition of shipyards, cement factories, and aluminum plants has been intricately intertwined with the fate of ministers, governments, and political agendas. The "politicization of the economy," which many observers of the present state of affairs point to as a source of problems and distortions, has originated largely from the presence of large firms in a small market.

A corollary to the limitations of size on the domestic market is that national growth, even if sparked by domestic factors, has always drawn sustenance from interlinkages with external markets and foreign economic relationships. This is reflected in the fact that Greece's economy has been an outward-looking one throughout its independent statehood, selling cash crops, labor, maritime and commercial services, raw materials, cheap manufactures, natural beauty, and archeological attractions to foreigners. It is also evident from the fact that both episodes of growth in the Greek economy during the twentieth century were curtailed because of international crises: the Great Depression of the late twenties and the first oil crisis of the mid-seventies. Quantitative support for this corollary can be found in the observation that during the protracted growth

---

1. National Statistical Service of Greece, *Census of Establishments 1988*, unpublished data quoted in V. Droucopoulos, D. Seremetis, and S. Thomadakis, *Globalization of Economic Activities and Small and Medium-Sized Entreprise Development: Country Study—Greece*, OECD Report, March 1994, pp. 15–16.

phase of 1960 to 1973 (the period hailed by many as the "Greek economic miracle"), gross domestic product grew at an average annual rate of 7.7 percent, but exports of goods and services grew at the much higher average rate of 12.6 percent. Parenthetically, both rates were the highest in Europe at the time, and the second highest among all OECD countries, after Japan.[2]

Although rarely considered by economic analysts, Greece's geographic location has also been an obstacle to economic growth. Its distance from large European markets—surely the longest among members of the European Union—creates a disadvantage not experienced by its partners. Moreover, Greece's natural trading hinterland to the north has been cut off throughout the postwar period by a frontier coincident with the iron curtain. The only passage through that frozen frontier, erstwhile Yugoslavia, became a war zone in the early 1990s. Greece's other natural trading hinterland, to the east, has also been virtually closed, for the Middle East has been a zone of antagonism and war, and Turkey is Greece's major military-political adversary. Thus, Greece is unique among European Union (EU) members in that it has enjoyed far fewer economic contacts with, and benefits from, its neighboring countries than any other member state of the European Union.

Greece's location in an area of festering antagonisms has acted as an indirect obstacle to economic growth by imposing on the country the necessity of high military expenditures. During the postwar peacetime, Greece has been spending an estimated 5.5 to 7 percent of its gross domestic product (GDP) on its military, more than any other European country. Had even half this amount been devoted to domestic investment instead of military expenses, Greece's long-term investment rate would have exceeded the European average, whereas in fact it fell short of that average over the long 1960–93 interval.[3]

Precisely because of these obstacles, "the Greek economic miracle"—the postwar episode of economic growth from 1958 to

---

2. OECD, *Historical Statistics* (1995 edition), Tables 3.1 and 4.8.

3. Gross fixed capital formation (i.e., aggregate investment) in relation to GDP over 1960–93 was 22.2 percent for EU members and 21.2 percent for Greece. An addition of 3.5 points to the Greek figure would have propelled Greece to the top five investment performers among EU members. See OECD, ibid., Table 6.8.

1973—was an exceptional achievement for Greece. It is worth sketching its main features. Table 1 offers a comparative summary.

Three observations derived from these data will suffice as background for the subsequent discussion. First, the four indicators depicting growth rates—GDP, export, industrial productivity, and investment—are all higher than the comparable international averages, testifying to sustained high performance of the Greek economy. The high concurrent rates of GDP, productivity, exports, and investment indicate a healthy and internally consistent process of growth that sustained itself for a considerable period of time. Especially notable, along with rapid growth, Greece experienced lower

TABLE 1

Indices of Performance 1960–73:
Greece, EU countries, OECD (% Annual Averages)

	GREECE	EU15	OECD
GDP growth	7.7	4.7	4.9
Export growth	12.6	8.1	8.0
Industrial productivity growth	6.6	5.5	4.1
Investment growth	10.0	5.5	6.2
Inflation rate (1963–73)	3.3	4.5	4.1
Unemployment rate	4.6	2.3	3.2
Public surplus (% GDP)	-1.2[a]	-0.2	-0.2
Trade surplus (% GDP)	-8.5	-0.5	0.0
Current account surplus (% GDP)[b]	-2.9	-0.1	0.1

Source: OECD, Historical Statistics (1995 edition).
[a]Author's estimate.
[b]This is a broader measure of external transactions than the trade surplus, because it includes "invisibles," such as emigrant remittances and profit repatriations.

than average inflation. In effect, growth and exceptional monetary stability were the characteristic macroeconomic features of the "Greek miracle."

Second, the last four indicators shown in Table 1 summarize the structural features of the Greek economy: public sector deficits, trade deficits, current account deficits, and unemployment rate as a percentage of the labor force. These measurements reveal moderate imbalances that apparently were not sufficient to put a brake on growth; nevertheless, they were higher than the comparable international levels. Specifically, the Greek public deficit and the current account deficit—both considered major macroeconomic indicators of structural growth constraints—were within very reasonable limits for a rapidly growing economy. On the other hand, the Greek trade deficit and the unemployment rate—each indicative of deeper structural conditions—were at considerable variance with comparable international levels. The large trade deficit reflected chiefly the need for imports of investment goods and industrial materials; this imbalance was itself an outcome of the domestic industrial weaknesses discussed earlier.

The third comment addresses the hidden but real importance of the Greek unemployment rate. The rate of 4.6 percent shown in Table 1 is moderate by present-day standards; yet, it appeared despite rapid growth and signaled the inability of the domestic economy to absorb labor as quickly as it was becoming available. This was due to two fundamental mechanisms: the release of workers from the agricultural sector, and the entry of women into the labor force. Perhaps the most fundamental structural feature of the "Greek miracle" was the potential for much higher unemployment, which translated into high emigration of labor, mostly to Germany. This high emigration soon resulted in a flow of remittances, which went to support the current account balance during the intensive phase of growth.

Greek Performance since 1974

The year 1974 marks a milestone in recent Greek history, for it witnessed the confluence of major economic and political changes. After the first oil crisis, the world economy was suddenly very different, and so was the Greek economy. The collapse of the military dictatorship in mid-1974 brought radical changes in Greek politics as well. The fledgling Greek democracy faced a daunting task. It had to survive and consolidate its political future in the midst of two crises: a foreign policy emergency as Turkey invaded Cyprus, and a major economic crisis as inflation, which had remained somewhat below 5 percent until 1972, shot up to 16 percent in 1973, and 27 percent in 1974. Greek total output had declined by 3.6 percent in 1974. Despite these problems, in my view, a second "Greek miracle" ensued, this time in the sphere of politics. A smooth transition to democracy and the establishment of a political system that had secured constitutional order and stable government was the achievement of this second "miracle."

Unfortunately, this splendid political achievement was not matched by economic performance. Summary data on growth and inflation rates for Greece, Spain, Portugal, and the fifteen EU countries are shown in Table 2 and they are revealing. All over Europe, the first oil crisis led to a retardation in growth and a jump in inflation. The three Mediterranean countries (Greece, Spain, and Portugal) were undergoing political transitions during this period and so suffered these effects in a more exaggerated way. This is evident by their higher rates of inflation in the 1970s. However, through the 1980s and early 1990s, Spain first and later Portugal regrouped, gaining both a rate of growth better than the European average rate of growth and considerable control over domestic inflation. Greece did not show comparable adjustment over the same period. Its growth rate remained lower and its inflation rate higher

TABLE 2

GDP Growth Rates (Gr.) and Inflation Rates (Inf.)

	1973–79		1979–84		1984–89		1989–93	
	Gr.	Inf.	Gr.	Inf.	Gr.	Inf.	Gr.	Inf.
Greece	3.7	16.1	0.8	21.8	2.8	17.0	0.9	17.5
Spain	2.3	18.3	1.4	13.6	4.2	6.8	1.4	5.8
Portugal	2.9	23.7	1.3	22.7	4.7	12.3	1.6	10.0
EU15	2.5	12.0	1.1	10.0	3.3	4.8	1.2	4.6

Source: OECD, Historical Statistics (1986, 1995 editions).

than that of both Mediterranean countries and the European average. Greece's domestic inflation rate is only now coming under control.[4] This delayed adjustment indicates a syndrome of economic malaise that requires further interpretation. It is nevertheless clear that Greece's condition of low growth and high inflation signals its disadvantages *vis-à-vis* its Mediterranean neighbors and its European partners.

Turning now to more detailed indicators of performance, we can examine the development of exports, investment, industrial productivity, and exchange rates over the post-1974 interval, shown in Table 3. Export figures can be considered an index of success in selling a country's products and services abroad. Greek exports have shown consistent vitality, growing at much higher rates than the exports of other countries shown, except for the interval 1979–84. (The slow export growth of that particular interval was caused by the maintenance of an overvalued drachma relative to growing domestic inflation. The devaluations of 1983 and 1985 realigned the currency.) Hence, export performance over the last decade justifies optimism, especially in view of the conclusions to be drawn from the remaining indicators of performance. It is fair to say that Greece's export sector retains resilience and the ability to maintain markets despite other obstacles.

The next two indices, growth of aggregate investment and growth of industrial productivity, seek to capture sources of growth and competitiveness. Investment and industrial productivity growth are generally thought of as necessary elements in a country's success to fuel its own economic growth and to compete with other countries. In both these aspects, Greece's performance has lagged behind its Mediterranean neighbors and the average performance of its fifteen EU partners. Especially worrisome is the slow growth of investment, which has not been sufficient in the last decade to counterbalance the negative growth of the previous decade. One probable outcome is precisely the lag we observe in growth of industrial productivity. This is perhaps the most ominous sign for the economic future of Greece. Reversal of sluggishness in investment and productivity should be central goals of Greek economic policy and institutional reform.

---

4. At year end 1995, the annual rate of change in the Greek CPI was about 8 percent.

Finally, we can interpret the exchange rate in Table 3 as an index of the purchasing power of Greek currency in the outside world, represented here by the U.S. dollar. The table shows that Greek currency has suffered much higher devaluation than currencies of other southern European countries. This primarily reflects the faster pace of Greek inflation (as we saw in Table 2). In fact, over the long term, the drachma/dollar exchange rate has slightly underadjusted for the inflation differential between Greece and the

TABLE 3

Average Annual Rates of Change in Exports, Exchange
Rates, Investment, and Industrial Productivity

		1973–79	1979–84	1984–89	1989–93
Export Volume	Greece	8.5	2.7	8.3	8.2
	Spain	5.7	7.4	3.8	6.6
	Portugal	1.5	8.5	5.9	2.8
	EU15	4.9	3.3	4.7	4.1
Aggregate Investment	Greece	-0.2	-4.5	2.6	1.0
	Spain	-1.2	-1.4	10.6	-1.9
	Portugal	-0.4	-2.1	7.5	2.4
	EU15	0.1	-0.7	5.5	-0.8
Industrial Productivity	Greece	1.2	-1.1	2.3	1.8
	Spain	3.1	5.4	1.2	2.5
	Portugal	n.a.	n.a.	n.a.	n.a.
	EU15	2.9	2.6	2.4	1.9
Exchange Rate (per US$)	Greece	-4.2	-40.9	-8.8	-10.3
	Spain	-2.5	-27.9	+5.3	-1.9
	Portugal	-16.6	-39.8	-1.5	-0.5
	DM	+6.3	-11.1	+6.8	+3.0

Source: OECD, Historical Statistics (1995 edition). (n.a. = not available.)

United States. Thus, it would appear that no strong competitive advantage has accrued to Greek exports over long periods on account of the exchange rate. On the other hand—and this point should be made—currencies acquire a "reputation" of their own as either stable or unstable, and this reputation contributes to preferences for assets denominated in those currencies. The drachma, because of its rapid nominal devaluations (seen in Table 3), is a currency of low reputation. The relatively new, and so far successfully pursued, monetary policy of three years that emphasizes a "strong drachma" seeks to reverse that cumulative negative reputation.[5]

Elements of Economic Structure

Assessments of performance must always be informed by readings of economic structure. The internal layout of an economy is important as a determinant of (or constraint on) performance. An economy's degree of "openness" to foreign trade, the relative weight of its industry, and its average rate of unemployment are important structural features having implications for performance. Table 4 offers a brief presentation of these.

The data on structure show, first, that Greece constitutes an open economy engaging in foreign trade equivalent to the European average. It is worth noting that beginning in the 1980s, Greek openness to trade exhibited a large quantitative increase, reflecting largely the creation of new trade opportunities after Greece joined the European Community in 1981.[6] Second, Greece is considerably less industrialized than its average European partner, and substantially less industrialized than Spain and Portugal, with which it is often compared. This lack of industrialization has handicapped Greece, because a less-industrialized economy has less capacity to absorb technology and generate advances in productivity. It could prove to be a source of opportunity, however, inasmuch as Greece

---

5. The policy is a relatively recent one and does not show its mark in the data of Table 3. See on this issue, Bank of Greece, *Report of the Governor* (Athens, 1995).

6. For an extensive analysis of the Greek economy in connection with the EU, see T. Giannitsis, *The Economy of Greece in the Perspective of the Single Market* (Stiftung Wissenschaft und Politik, SWP S 388, August 1993).

TABLE 4

Relation of Performance to Economic Structure:
Openness to Trade, Industry Contribution, Unemployment

		1974–79	1980–84	1985–89	1990–93
Imports+Exports to GDP (%)	Greece	42.7	47.7	55.8	55.2
	Spain	31.1	38.8	40.2	38.1
	Portugal	49.7	75.8	57.2	65.1
	EU15	50.0	54.2		52.8
Industry Value-added to GDP (%)	Greece	27.3	26.4	25.8	23.0
	Spain	36.5	33.7	39.9	33.1
	Portugal	39.1	39.3	38.4	n.a.
	EU15	38.6	35.0		31.6
Unemployment Rate (%)	Greece	1.9	5.7	6.3	8.3
	Spain	5.3	16.6	18.4	18.1
	Portugal	6.0	7.9	6.7	4.7
	EU15	4.6	9.2		9.4

Source: OECD, Historical Statistics (1986 and 1995 editions).

has fewer resources frozen in obsolete industrial assets. Finally, Greece's rate of unemployment is rapidly converging on the European average, a worrisome situation for a country less industrialized than the average European country. It is a harbinger of intensifying social problems around the issues of work, income, and welfare. One broad point can be gleaned from a correlation of the performance data and structural features presented in Table 4: a small but open economy with low industrialization, like the Greek economy, is likely to be quite sensitive to economic cycles and events occurring in the international sphere. Thus, Greece cannot engineer its recovery or sustain growth on its own. It can only do so within a stable and prosperous international environment.

The Public Sector

One special element of the economy deserves separate treatment because it touches on both performance and structure: the Greek public sector. The public sector has been demonized by some as the main culprit in Greek economic problems. It has been seen by "liberals" as the source of all evil and by "statists" as the source of all solutions. A cooler view of the Greek public sector must take into account a few historical facts, and some data.

The state has always played a significant role in the Greek economy. The two growth episodes of the twentieth century coincided with periods of increasing intervention by the state. Especially in the aftermath of the Second World War, heavy regulation of the economy was seen as a method for making order out of chaos.[7] Notably, the "economic miracle" of the 1960s unfolded under very strict government regulation of consumer prices, interest rates, credit, and investment selection. The success story of state intervention always had a dark side, however. The regulatory mechanisms were invariably in danger of completely eroding and being turned into instruments of political favoritism. This erosion was most obvious during the military dictatorship, which granted favors without fear of political opposition.

The major failure of regulatory mechanisms became apparent during the economic crisis in the mid-1970s, when the state sought to shield various groups against its effects. Attempts to protect farmers, wage earners, and pensioners by means of mandated income increases, as well as steps taken to support failing industry through the regulation of banks, only served to fuel inflation without stimulating growth. The use of regulatory intervention in the economy also had negative political consequences. It created stakeholders, who mounted strong political resistance when liberalization was attempted. It also created a contest among social groups for the acquisition of protection by the state. This contest

---

7. See S.B. Thomadakis, "Stabilization, Development and Government Economic Authority in the 1940s," in J.O. Iatrides and L. Wrigley, eds., *Greece at the Crossroads: The Civil War and Its Legacy* (University Park, Penn.: Pennsylvania State University Press, 1995), pp. 173–226. For Greek financial regulation, see D. Halikias, *Money and Credit in a Developing Economy: The Greek Case* (New York: New York University Press, 1978).

TABLE 5
Fiscal Magnitudes As Percent of GDP

PANEL A: Fiscal Balances

		1974–79	1980–84	1985–89	1990–93
Current Expenditure	Greece	28.0	36.0	45.2	49.7
	Spain	23.6	32.0	36.1	40.1
	Portugal	29.1	36.5	39.1	n.a.
	EU15	39.3	44.8		46.7
Current Receipts	Greece	29.1	31.4	35.4	38.8
	Spain	25.7	31.6	36.2	39.2
	Portugal	27.6	34.8	37.6	n.a.
	EU15	39.7	43.5		44.6
Surplus	Greece	+1.1	-4.6	-9.8	-10.9
	Spain	+2.1	-0.4	+0.1	-0.9
	Portugal	-1.5	-1.7	-1.5	n.a.
	EU15	+0.4	-1.3		-2.1

PANEL B: Structure of Taxes

		1975	1980	1985	1991
Income and Social Security Taxes	Greece		8.7	10.5	9.8
	Spain		7.5	7.8	10.1
	Portugal		7.3	9.0	9.9
	EU15		14.3	15.1	15.3
Corporate and Property Taxes	Greece		6.6	7.1	8.5
	Spain		11.4	11.4	13.3
	Portugal		7.1	7.6	9.7
	EU15		10.6	11.4	11.2
Indirect Taxes	Greece		12.1	15.0	17.4
	Spain		5.0	8.3	9.8
	Portugal		12.9	13.5	14.9
	EU15		11.3	12.4	12.9
Total Taxes	Greece	25.5	27.4	32.6	35.7
	Spain	19.4	23.9	27.5	33.2
	Portugal	24.7	27.3	30.1	34.5
	EU15	33.0	36.2	38.9	39.4

Sources: OECD, Historical Statistics (1986 and 1995 editions) and Revenue Statistics.

created pressures for an ever-widening supply of state grants and fed the structural fiscal deficits.

To reconstruct and consolidate a viable democracy can be a long-drawn-out and costly project. Part of the consolidation process, in the case of Greece, resulted in the emergence of two major parties that would compete and occasionally alternate in power. This auspicious political outcome was in the making for about ten years after the change in 1974. It required that sufficiently large masses of the electorate be persuaded to play the bipartisan game, and this meant in turn that economic policy became an instrument for manipulating the electorate. Thus, the consolidation of democracy in Greece became coincident with the consolidation of a bipartisan system in politics. In the process, the two large parties practiced a brand of competitive politics that gave rise to two fundamental causes of fiscal impasse: postponement of tax reform and the emergence of an electoral-fiscal cycle. The evolution of Greek fiscal conditions is marked by these fundamental flaws. These can be seen in inter-temporal and comparative perspective in the data of Table 5.

Panel A of Table 5 shows fiscal expenditures and receipts as a percentage of GDP.[8] Panel B presents elements indicative of comparable tax structures. The data enable us to make three observations. First, in terms of spending and taxing patterns, the three Mediterranean countries were similar and started from a lower level of fiscal activity than the average European country. In terms of formal fiscal size, states in southern Europe have traditionally been smaller than in the north. However, over the last two decades, the Mediterranean states have been converging on the European average, on both the spending and the taxing side. Second, Greece shows a large divergence of expenditures from tax revenues, especially in the last decade. This fiscal imbalance is not typical of the other Mediterranean countries. Greece's imbalance has been growing, whereas the imbalance of the other two countries has remained steady. This unique condition is underscored by the fact that since 1985, Greece has experienced a spiral of accumulating public debt, increasing interest payments, and swelling deficits. Third, and most interesting, is that tax burdens in Greece have grown in tandem with those of its Mediterranean neighbors; Greece's

---

8. For reasons of data comparability, the expenditure shown in Table 5 excludes public investment.

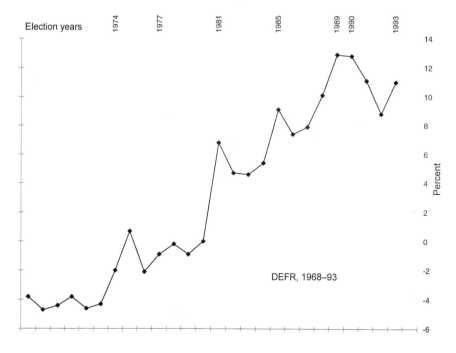

Figure 1. Public Deficit to GDP Ratio (DEFR), Greece, 1968–93.

peculiarity is its much greater dependence on indirect taxation. In my view, this peculiarity reflects the absence of significant tax reform over the period studied. The pressure for collecting revenue has been relieved by the expedient of higher indirect taxes. This strategy has been politically more expedient, but less than satisfactory in terms of a contribution to efficiency and economic growth.

Finally, it is enlightening to look at the development of Greek public deficits over time and the evidence of their political impact on the economy through electoral-fiscal cycles. Figure 1 shows the deficit (as a ratio of GDP) from 1968 to 1993. Each peak shown in the diagram, after 1974, is associated with an election. The first two peaks occurred the year after election years, in 1975 and 1978. The remaining five peaks occurred in election years 1981, 1985, 1989, 1990, and 1993. The regularity is statistically significant.[9] Every election year has added an average 1.83 percent of GDP to the public deficit. The effects of these cycles have been detrimental in several respects, including an erosion of confidence in the integrity of the state.[10]

In the 1990s, the public sector has undergone considerable change that is not yet evident in the statistics. Substantial deregulation, limited privatization of publicly owned enterprises, and significant steps toward tax reform have been effected. Data from the last two years indicate a stabilization of inflationary trends and the level of public debt. Still, the accumulated burden of past deficits will make Greek public finances precarious for some time. Given the challenges of development and competitiveness that Greece will continue to face in the future as a member of the European Union, the Greek public sector might have the following desiderata:

1. Persistence in the implementation of tax reform, so that tax burdens become more evenly distributed across income and social grown classes. Tax reform must include development of major

---

9. This result comes from a linear regression of deficit ratios (DEFR) against a time factor (T), and an election-year dummy variable (ELY). The resulting estimation yielded: DEFR = $-7.34 + 0.74T + 1.83ELY$. The coefficient of ELY is statistically significant at the 5 percent level, and the R-squared of the regression is 0.92.

10. See S. Thomadakis and D. Seremetis, "Fiscal Management, Social Agenda, and Structural Deficits," in T. Kariotis, ed., *The Greek Socialist Experiment: Papandreou's Greece 1981–1989* (New York: Pella, 1992), pp. 203–255.

grown classes. Tax reform must include development of major policies in problem areas such as illegal trade, contraband, and tax evasion. Tax reform and enforcement are necessary ingredients in a reconstruction of the credibility of the tax system.

2. Rapid substitution of modern forms of public intervention for more outdated methods in areas of market oversight, competition, quality regulation, and the development of rules governing a variety of areas, including bankruptcy procedures, mergers, educational credentials, and accounting norms.

3. Provision of effective economic coordination, where coordination is understood to mean a policy framework within which private and nonprivate initiatives can unfold, but in ways that are mutually reinforcing and supporting. Coordination, as a public good, can increase the effectiveness of private initiatives. The need for this public good became apparent during the years following the first and second "Delors packages," which have transferred large sums from the European Union for structural initiatives in Greece.

4. Development of political arrangements (e.g., interparty agreements, nonpolitical appointments at the finance ministry) for the elimination of the electoral-fiscal cycle.

5. As a corollary of (4), movement forward on radical reform of the Greek public welfare system. The absence of effective institutions of social protection in Greece is in part responsible for the emergence of these political cycles, which have left negative marks on both Greek economics and politics. The reform of the Greek system of social services and welfare must be founded on two basic principles. First, a stable and credible mechanism of provision must be constructed that will not be politically negotiable or contestable. Second, the credibility of the system must be guaranteed by a double-barreled policy to both streamline programs to real needs and secure tax revenues for its maintenance.

6. Development of a judicious but credible policy of privatization of public sector enterprises. Looking at the Greek public sector above and beyond basic government services, even a casual observer can see remnants of the past: a mixture of public entrepreneurial activities that arose either from past takeovers of firms in crisis or from demands for public goods that were meaningful in earlier decades but that are now obsolete at current income levels and living standards. Despite the plenitude of government-run enterprises, there is a lack of public goods and services appropriate for a state with Greece's current configuration of incomes, living

standards, and social needs. Decongestion of urban services, maintenance of a heretofore deteriorating natural environment, and the provision of continuing education and training programs are public services that are still embryonic in their development in Greece. Thus, policies of privatization must to be designed and pursued in the context of a more general strategy for the modernization of the public sector.

The Financial Sector

Since 1987, the Greek financial sector has undergone almost complete liberalization. It has also exhibited a strong, positive performance both in terms of activity growth and in terms of product development, quality of service, and innovation. It has been an area of the economy that has finally received, and continues to receive, infusions of foreign capital. The original impetus for financial reform in Greece was the initiative of then–Deputy Minister of National Economy Theodore Karatzas, who sponsored a report recommending the liberalization of the financial sector. Soon afterwards, both the government and the Central Bank began a movement toward deregulation that revitalized Greek's financial services industry.

Focusing on changes in the banking system first, interest rates are now determined by the market, quantity controls on credit have long been abolished, foreign exchange markets and cross-border capital movements have been deregulated, and opportunities for entry into banking have been opened. In the early 1980s, fewer than twenty banks operated in Greece; today almost fifty banks are in business, making entry into banking one of the more impressive outcomes of deregulation. European Union directives on the freedom to establish banks in other member countries, on the freedom to provide financial services across borders, and on common standards for the safety of banks' capital are now being implemented in Greece, as in other countries of the European Union. In short, banking is becoming a very competitive business in Greece. Its modernization is obvious both in terms of a big change in the quality of banking services and the growth of skilled jobs in the banking sector.

The Athens Stock Exchange (ASE) has also undergone significant modernization and revitalization since 1987. Legislation enabling the formation of brokerage firms and their participation as members of the exchange, the introduction of an automated trading system, and the establishment of the Central Securities Depository have been the main institutional changes of recent years. Market capitalization of the shares listed in 1993 was $13.5 billion, and the total value of transactions was $2.8 billion. Since 1990, there have been fifty-seven new listings, bringing the total number of companies with listed stocks to 150 at the end of 1993. New capital raised in 1993 through stock issues amounted to $436 million.[11]

The modernization of the Greek financial system has included the introduction of mutual funds. In 1990, only seven funds were available to Greek investors with total assets of Dr 147 billion. By the end of 1994, 98 funds were available with total assets nine times larger. These were also available in a great variety of investment choices, comprising, figuratively, baskets of domestic stocks, bonds, and foreign securities.[12]

Policies in the financial area are directed mainly at the maintenance of competition in banking and further strengthening the role of the stock exchange. Competition in banking appears increasingly to take the form of the introduction of new products and services. For example, automated teller machines (ATMs), recently introduced by one or two market leaders, have now forced most banks to establish similar facilities. Increased competition among banks creates the need for enhanced banking supervision. Modern supervision of banks is being designed and implemented by the Central Bank, and an insurance deposit program has recently been put in place.[13] Moreover, an initiative is underway to create an automated interbank clearing and payments system in Greece.

Plans to enhance the stock exchange are proceeding along two axes: introduction of trading in derivatives and linkage of ASE with peripheral terminals, in Thessaloniki, for example. Encouraging

---

11. Athens Stock Exchange, *Yearbook* (various years; in Greek).

12. See E. Gatzonas, "Tendencies and Prospects in the Sector of Mutual Funds," and N. Milonas, "Mutual Funds in Greece: Risk, Return and Evaluation in the Period 1990–94," both in G. Provopoulos, ed., *The Greek Financial System: Tendencies and Prospects* (in Greek) (Athens, 1995).

13. The Greek Deposit Insurance Fund was created by Law 2324/95 and insures depositors in line with European Union guidelines for sums up to 20,000 ECU.

foreign companies, especially in the Balkans, to list their shares on the exchange is also an immediate goal. More generally, the extension of Greek financial services into the neighboring Balkan countries is an active policy goal, with several Greek banks already having established foreign branches. Furthermore, an internationally sponsored credit institution, the Bank of Black Sea Countries, is currently being established in Thessaloniki.

It is clear that the momentum for change and growth in the financial sector is being kept alive in Greece both at the level of competitive financial firms and their initiatives and at the level of policy, where it is essential to continue to formulate institutional arrangements that guarantee safe and sound banking and smoothly working financial markets.

Conclusion: What Can Be Expected in the Future?

Is it paradoxical to be optimistic about Greek economic prospects after acknowledging the lackluster performance of the past twenty years? It is not. Besides the well-known capacities of the Greeks, there are many examples of good performance to be found despite the general poor performance, there are changes in traditional geoeconomic obstacles that present new opportunities for Greece, and there are signs of a collective will to learn from the economic lessons of the last two decades.

The financial sector is not unique as a model of achievement. An emerging number of cases in the manufacturing and service sectors indicate that there is a healthy economic segment which has undergone adjustment and which can become and remain internationally competitive. Success stories in traditional sectors such as food and textiles, and in nontraditional sectors such as business and financial consulting, have started to counter the stories of failure that have been common since the 1970s.

The opening of areas in the Balkans and the Black Sea, and the contemplation of a peaceful Yugoslav region, eliminate an important and historical geoeconomic obstacle to Greek development. A host of economic opportunities, which are already being exploited by Greek entrepreneurs, have opened up and more are expected in the future. However, these new initiatives call for new state intervention. A variety of institutional arrangements are needed to facilitate the security and freedom of payments and capital movements in the broader area of the Balkans and the Black Sea. Important issues of migration also require the formulation of new policies and mechanisms of enforcement.

Collective learning from recent economic history and low performance is apparent in several respects. Recently, for the first time, there appears to be agreement virtually across the political spectrum that economic stabilization must precede the satisfaction of social demands. The behavior of collective bodies such as employers and employee organizations has moderated a great deal and is now bent on convergence. Recent success in reducing inflation is not only the outcome of fiscal policy. It results from employee-employer consensus about income growth and a more general social consensus in support of stabilization. Thus, social learning is evident both at the level of political parties and at the level of "civil society."

One critical failure that has prevented individual abilities from translating into collective performance in the economy is the lack of effective coordination and policy continuity. The benefits of collective learning must translate not only into modifications in the behavior of governments, social groups, and consumers, but also into a new set of modern institutional arrangements that create market regulation and policy cohesiveness. Greece's antiquated and fragmented institutional arrangements are themselves a major obstacle to development. Pressure from the European Union has been a major factor so far in bringing about institutional change. Yet, the unique conditions in Greece and its recent history of poor economic performance require changes more far reaching than those mandated by the European Union. It is always a solid reminder that the many successes of the Greeks of the diaspora are to no small degree the outcome of a combination of their entrepreneurial abilities with advanced institutional arrangements not of their own making, which encouraged the development of strategic action and the diminution of politically driven uncertainties.

Chapter 4

Monteagle Stearns

Greek Security Issues

The Greek paradox in the field of security is not between Greece's military performance and its military potential, but between its military performance and its diplomatic and economic potential.

Aristotle wrote that the defenders of a walled city have a choice of strategies. Either they can defend the city as walled or as unwalled. The defenders of a city without walls, however, have no choice. A forward defense is their only feasible strategy.[1]

This is roughly the strategic situation of Greece today. Ancient Greece was protected by the hazardous winds and currents of the Aegean and the "wooden walls" of the Greek fleet, as well as by the massive ashlar fortifications of its cities. Modern Greece enjoys no such advantages. Its natural defenses have been drastically reduced by advances in military technology, but the scope of its defensive perimeter has not. Greece must still provide for the defense not only of the Greek mainland and the Peloponnesus but of fifteen hundred Greek islands scattered across the Ionian and Aegean seas from the coast of Albania to the coast of Turkey. Under the common defense policy to which Athens has committed itself with Nicosia, the Greek defensive perimeter now extends to the Republic of Cyprus, over five hundred miles to the southeast of the Greek mainland. Cyprus aside, the coastline of Greece, including its islands, is close to that of the contiguous coastal border of the United States.[2] While Greek land frontiers extend only 725 miles, they are penetrated by north-south river valleys, like the Vardar and Struma, which have

---

Monteagle Stearns served as U.S. Ambassador to Greece, 1981–85.

1. Aristotle, *Politics, Book VII*, 11 91331-15.

2. The Greek coastline is 13,676 km and that of the United States is 19,924 km. Source: *CIA World Factbook, 1995–96*, pp. 154, 416.

facilitated the passage of invading armies three times in the twentieth century. This is the sense in which modern Greece resembles Aristotle's unwalled city and is the reason why the central question for Greece's defenders is not whether to adopt a forward defensive strategy but what kind of forward strategy will best provide for Greek security.

The question cannot be answered in military terms alone. Greece has a population of 10.6 million and its armed forces number 159,300, clearly too few in themselves to patrol and defend the entire Greek perimeter. Since modern Greece declared its independence in 1821, astute diplomacy has been as important as military strength in securing Greek frontiers. The choice of allies and the structure of alliances are vital components of Greece's defense strategy. The imperatives driving the strategy arise from Greece's position as both a Balkan and a Mediterranean country. The strategic choice defined by geography for Greek political leaders has usually been narrow: whether to align Greece with the land power dominant on the Balkan peninsula or the sea power dominant in the Mediterranean.

The history of modern Greece shows that its leaders turn their backs on the sea at their peril. Both the Crimean War and World War I resulted in the occupation of Greek ports by the British and French when Greece sided with, or was feared to be siding with, the dominant land power in the region, Russia in the first case, Germany in the second. Even the Greek civil war of 1944–49 can be interpreted as a choice between land-based and sea-based alliances, since the Greek government was aligned with the sea power dominant in the Mediterranean, represented by the future members of NATO, and the Greek Communists with the land power dominant on the Balkan peninsula, represented by the future members of the Warsaw Pact.

The defeat of the Greek Communists in 1949 and the entry of Greece into NATO three years later seemed to settle the question of whether Greek defenses would be land- or sea-oriented for the duration of the Cold War. As far as NATO was concerned, the principal threat to Greek security came from the north. Greece's NATO mission was to defend its northern and northwestern borders from Communist attack, provide port and communications facilities for the U.S. Sixth Fleet, and coordinate the air and sea defenses of the Aegean and the Dardanelles with Turkey. To support that mission, and ostensibly to support Greek-Turkish military cooperation in defense of NATO's southeastern flank, Greece received over $7 billion worth of military aid from the United States and from NATO infrastructure funds between 1949 and 1995. In the same period, Greece's NATO ally, Turkey, received over $10 billion in military aid.[3]

In reality, starting in 1955, Greek and NATO defense doctrines began increasingly to diverge. Greek-Turkish tensions arising from the commencement that year of negotiations in London on independence for Cyprus, and the anti-Greek riots in Istanbul and Izmir engineered by the Turkish government in September 1955, to forestall independence, spelled the beginning of the end for effective military cooperation between Greece and Turkey. The actual end came in the summer of 1974 when a bungled coup d'état against the Cypriot government, mounted by the Greek military junta then in power in Athens, opened the door to Turkish occupation of northern Cyprus, where 30,000 Turkish troops still remain.

Since that time—fifteen years before the Berlin Wall was breached—no Greek government has accorded a higher priority to Greece's northern (land) defenses than to its eastern (sea) defenses. No Greek government has seen a threat to Greek security more dangerous than the threat perceived from Turkey. Greek and NATO defense doctrines not only diverged in the last fifteen years of the Cold War, they became antithetical. Instead of directly addressing Greek-Turkish differences, however, NATO tended to disparage their importance while trying to limit their impact on the alliance's planning and operations. As a result of this neglect, tensions between the two allies increased and began to affect an ever-wider range of NATO activities, including some, like arms-control negotiations with the Soviet Union, whose strategic significance extended far beyond the southeastern flank.

Given their differing perceptions of where the main threat to Greek security lay, it is not surprising that the collapse of the Warsaw Pact and the Soviet Union was less disorienting for Greece than for NATO. Greek defense planners, unlike their counterparts

---

3. Thus maintaining the 7:10 ratio in U.S. military aid to Greece and Turkey that has come to be accepted as meeting the provisions of the 1961 Foreign Assistance Act, which specifies that military aid to the two countries must be "designed to insure that the present balance of military strength among the countries of the region ... is preserved." Section 620(b) of the Foreign Assistance Act of 1961, as amended.

in Brussels, felt no need to reformulate defense policies, rethink their order of battle, or search for new missions to justify their existence. Conservative Greek governments had begun to cultivate cordial relations with the Warsaw Pact states in the 1970s. Prime Minister Constantine Karamanlis paid an official visit to Moscow in 1979. In the 1980s, Greek socialist governments continued the process of rapprochement. In Greek eyes, when NATO finally (and somewhat reluctantly) declared the Cold War to have ended, the main threat to Greece's security remained where it had always been, in the east. It was the collapse of Yugoslavia, not the Soviet Union, that disoriented Greece and continues to create the most difficult problems for Greek security.

The New Strategic Landscape

Yugoslavia's contribution to Greek security began in 1948 when Marshal Tito broke with Stalin while the Greek civil war was still in progress. Before that time, Tito had been a much more enthusiastic supporter of the Greek Communists than Stalin, and Yugoslavia had provided a privileged sanctuary and training ground for Communist guerilla forces. Tito's motive was territorial as much as ideological. He nominally supported the creation of an independent Macedonian state but clearly had in mind a satellite state that would incorporate northern Greece and extend Yugoslav influence to the Aegean. The break with Stalin forced Tito to abandon this objective and normalize relations with Greece. By closing the Yugoslav-Greek border, he fatally restricted the room for maneuver of the Greek Communist forces and enabled the Greek government to defeat them decisively in the Grammos mountains in the summer of 1949.

Although the "Macedonian question" was never entirely banished from the Greek mind, a nonaligned Yugoslavia under Tito's leadership seemed to assure that it would remain dormant during his lifetime. Indeed, until the Yugoslav federation's breakup in 1992, cultivation of good Greek-Yugoslav relations was as important to Athens as to Belgrade. The two states were even briefly allied militarily under the Bled agreement of 1954, which, however, withered away almost immediately as Belgrade's relations with Moscow improved after the death of Stalin.

For Greeks, the demise of Yugoslavia meant the rebirth of the Macedonian question, unmistakably so when Skopje declared itself the capital of an independent "Republic of Macedonia." Passionate Greek insistence that the new republic change its name, flag, and constitution before being accorded international recognition, and the Greek embargo imposed in 1994 to bring this about, were emphatic indications that Greeks had not forgotten that their civil war was, among other things, a struggle for control of northern Greece. Outside Greece, the reasons for Greek passion were poorly understood and poorly explained by Athens. Nevertheless, those in the United States in particular who have criticized Greeks for being swept away by nationalism might reflect on how American public opinion would react if the northeastern states of Mexico declared their independence under the name the "Republic of Texas," and raised a flag emblazoned with the Alamo.

Greek passion over the Macedonian issue is, in fact, easier to understand than the tactics Greece adopted to resolve the problem. The state that is internationally recognized as the "Former Yugoslav Republic of Macedonia" (FYROM) has a population of only 2.3 million inhabitants, of whom perhaps thirty percent are ethnically Albanian, Turkish, or Serbian. Tensions between the sizable Albanian minority and the Slav majority are a constant threat to the small state's internal stability. Landlocked, poor in natural resources, and afflicted with domestic divisions, the former Yugoslav republic, under whatever name, could only pose a threat to Greek security if backed by a larger power, such as Bulgaria, Serbia, or Turkey. Since the port of Thessaloniki is the nearest outlet for its exports, and Greece is its natural trading partner, Skopje's decisions in the field of foreign and security policy cannot fail to be strongly, indeed decisively influenced by Greece.

However, instead of capitalizing on this natural dependency to build closer relations (and even greater dependency), Greece took the opposite course and tried to isolate Skopje. The result was to push the new state into greater dependence on its other neighbors—exactly the situation Greece should have been trying to avoid. Turkish and Bulgarian influence in Skopje grew at the expense of Greek influence. Furthermore, the Greek embargo isolated Greece politically almost as much as it isolated FYROM economically. Fellow members of the European Union called on Greece to lift the embargo, and the United States, although in deference to Greek wishes, stopping short of sending an ambassador to Skopje, sought to persuade Greece to set aside the question of what the new state would be called. An agreement has finally been reached through U.S. mediation that enables Greece to end the embargo, but the name issue has been heavily politicized in Athens and Skopje, and Greece has lost much time that could have been used to better effect on problems more fundamental to Greek security.

The Macedonian question, and Greece's response to it, are illustrations of a point made earlier: military measures alone cannot defend Greek borders. When diplomatic policy results in the isolation of Greece and the weakening of its alliances, forward defense of Greek interests becomes increasingly difficult. In the case of the Yugoslav breakup, Greece's outspoken partisanship for the Serbs and its embargo against Skopje have limited Greek opportunities to play a more significant role in resolving the conflict, one that would better protect the country's long-term interests in the region and strengthen its influence in the European Union and NATO. In assessing strategic options for Greek policymakers in the future, including both the opportunities and dangers that exist in a changing strategic landscape, it is important to bear in mind that their diplomatic choices will be as important as their military ones.

Questions for the Future

Greece in the twenty-first century will still, of course, be a Balkan and a Mediterranean country. Its strategic choices will still be limited by its size and geography. There are, however, significant differences between Greece's strategic position throughout the nineteenth and most of the twentieth centuries, and its position as it approaches the twenty-first century. The most important is the result of Greece's greater political maturity. During much of the nineteenth century, foreign patrons were such a determining factor in Greek politics that the major parties were informally referred to as the "British," "French," and "Russian" parties. In the period from World War I to World War II, the political differences of royalists and Venizelists were easier to discern in their external than in their internal programs. The Greek civil war and the Cold War that followed it carried this process of "externalization" of Greek political life to its logical extreme.

Modern Greece needs allies but not patrons. Greek political parties may disagree about the identity of Greece's true friends and natural allies, but are not themselves defined by these disagreements. They represent, as they should, alternative approaches to the entire spectrum of internal and external policy choices confronting Greece. Accordingly, Greek political factionalism is less likely today than in the past to facilitate foreign intervention.

Another significant change in Greece's strategic position is the result of the changing balance of power in Europe. Unlike the situation prevailing in the nineteenth century, there are no major European powers with the motive or capability to dominate Greece strategically. Unlike the situation prevailing between World Wars I and II, Greece is a member of the two alliances whose success or failure will determine the power alignments of Europe in the next century. An effectively functioning NATO can bolster Greek security against external threats, and an effectively functioning European Union can strengthen the country's political and economic health against internal threats. Greece's principal concern should be to assure that its role is taken seriously by both organizations and that, in consequence, it can contribute to their viability. Although Greek geography imposes the need for strong national defenses, no amount of defense spending can provide the margin of security (and deterrence) afforded Greece by its system of alliances if they are in working order.

The Greek defense budget for 1995 (the most recent year for which figures are available)[4] projects Dr 772 billion ($3.38 billion) in defense expenditures. This would amount to about 4.6 percent of Greece's gross domestic product (GDP). The actual level of Greek defense expenditures, including loans and defense-related expenditures, is certainly much higher, probably in the range of Dr 1 trillion ($4.3 billion). This would represent almost six percent of GDP. Some estimates push the figure even higher, to over seven percent of GDP. Whichever number is correct, there is no doubt that Greek defense expenditures as a proportion of GDP are the highest among European members of NATO. Of the $4 billion or more Greece spent on defense in 1995, forty-seven percent went to the army, twenty-nine percent to the air force, and twenty-four percent to the navy. In terms of combat readiness, morale, and training, the Greek armed forces are among NATO's best. This has been true

---

4. These figures are taken from *The Military Balance, 1995–1996* (London: Brassey's for the International Institute for Strategic Studies, October 1995), pp. 50–52.

since Greece joined NATO in 1952, except, paradoxically, for the seven years Greece was ruled by a military junta that mismanaged the armed forces as badly as it did the country as a whole.

However, for a state struggling to reach the economic goals of the European Union, Greece spends more than it can afford on defense. As Stavros Thomadakis points out, "had even half the amount of these expenditures been devoted to domestic investment instead of military expense, Greece's long-term investment rate would have exceeded that of the European average, whereas in fact it fell short of that average over the long interval 1960–93."[5]

The Greek defense budget is also larger than it probably needs to be in a period when Greece faces no imminent military threat. The viability of the Greek economy as a component of Greece's security is no less important than its military readiness and the credibility of its alliances. Defense expenditures are, at their present levels, the single most important contributor to Greece's external debt. According to Defense Minister Gerassimos Arsenis, Greece spends about $1 billion annually on military imports, much of it financed by loans. It spends only five percent of that amount on procurement from the ailing Greek defense industry.[6] Just as the decision to extend Greece's security zone to Cyprus placed a heavy burden on Greece's defense posture, the decision to continue expending so large a proportion of GDP on defense places a heavy burden on the Greek economy. If Greece is to meet the European Union's convergence criteria within the next five years, the conclusion is inescapable that Greek defense expenditures will have to be significantly reduced. More cost-effective ways to assure national security will have to be found.

Greek preoccupation with Turkey and the need to maintain a balance of power in the Aegean are the main explanations for continued high levels of Greek defense spending. Bloodshed in Bosnia, the confrontation between Athens and Skopje, and troubled Greek relations with Albania are others. Bad rapport with Albania,

---

5. See Stavros B. Thomadakis, "The Greek Economy: Performance, Expectations, and Paradoxes," Chapter 3 in this volume.

6. Gerassimos Arsenis, "National Power and International Competitiveness," *Emphasis: A Journal of Hellenic Issues* (published by Hellenic Resources Institute) Vol. 1, No. 1 (April–June, 1995), pp. 10–24.

among its other effects, has complicated the task of controlling illegal immigration into Greece. The number of Albanian refugees is presently estimated to exceed 200,000, adding to Greek concerns about internal security and representing an additional drain on Greek resources. These regional preoccupations explain why the Greek approach to the larger issues of European security has tended to be parochial and piecemeal. Yet, paradoxically, it is through satisfactory resolution of these larger issues that Greece is likely to find a more cost-effective way to assure its own security from regional threats.

In general, Greece favors strengthening a European defense identity. Having become a full member of the Western European Union (WEU), the Greek government clearly (and correctly) sees its future in a closer security relationship with Western Europe. Its view of European defense planning resembles that of the French. There are, however, some limitations on the extent to which Greece can look to Western Europe for support in its regional disputes. This was signalled by the protocol WEU members attached to the article of Greek accession, making clear that the Brussels Treaty's mutual defense commitment would not apply in the case of a conflict between Greece and a fellow member of NATO (i.e., Turkey).[7] In addition, Greece does not wish deliberately to weaken its defense relationship with the United States. The most important Greek weapons systems, including the most technologically advanced, are American supplied, and the United States is sometimes more sensitive to Greek concerns than the Europeans, thereby providing a useful counterweight. Difficult choices will nevertheless present themselves to Greek policymakers, as they already have in the question of whether to upgrade the F-4s or F-16s of the Hellenic Air Force—a step necessitated, among other factors, by extension of the Greek defense perimeter to Cyprus, where these aircraft, as presently configured, have only a few minutes loiter time.[8] The F-4s

---

7. Article 5 of the Brussels Treaty states that the signatories will afford any member suffering aggression "all the military and other aid and resistance in their power."

8. Flying from the Greek mainland, an F-4 Phantom's loiter time over Cyprus is no more than one to two minutes. This was an important factor in the Greek government's decision in 1974 not to provide air support to Cypriot forces resisting Turkish landings on the north coast of Cyprus. Turkey also wants to upgrade its F-4s and has provoked some controversy in the Turkish military and among fundamentalist

can be upgraded in Germany, the F-16s only in the United States. The choice is complicated by the fact that Athens is seeking from Washington two additional squadrons of older F-16s (a total of forty aircraft) in exchange for doing the work in the United States. Nevertheless, Greece's decision will have an effect on future procurement policy and will be an indication of whether closer defense ties with Western Europe will be at the expense of existing ties with the United States.

On the question of NATO expansion to the east, the attitude of Athens is somewhat ambivalent. A desire to strengthen relations with its Eastern European neighbors discourages Greece from actively opposing expansion, but a desire to remain in step with Russia (which shares Greece's sympathy for the Serbs) prevents Athens from actively supporting expansion if Russia is excluded. EU expansion presents fewer problems for Greece, although it has a greater economic stake in expansion south than in expansion east. The top Greek priority goes to the accession of Cyprus, followed by that of Malta, which would also strengthen the Mediterranean bloc in the European Union. Expansion east is supported by Greece as long as it does not adversely affect the interests of the southern EU members by diverting attention from their needs and diminishing the regional funds available to meet them.

If there is a defect in Greece's approach to the larger issues of European security, it is a defect inherent in reactive policies: being defensive in nature, the policies are designed to prevent undesirable outcomes rather than to secure desirable ones; being aimed at short-term problems, their lasting impact is negligible. All the European states who attended the 1996 EU Intergovernmental Conference (IGC) on the future of the European Union have serious thinking to do. Greek preparations should include more thought on what kind of "deepening" and what kind of "broadening" of European defense, economic, and political structures will best serve Greece's longer-term interests. A more focused examination of the overall issues to be discussed at the IGC would not only clarify their implications for Greece but might strengthen Greek influence at the conference. So far, there seems to have been little consideration

---

groups by awarding a contract to upgrade 54 Phantoms to Israel Aircraft Industries (IAI).

given to these long-term issues by either the Greek government or the opposition.

Part of the effort to think through Greece's future place in Europe should be an effort to develop new approaches to the problem of Greek-Turkish relations. The Greek government showed the value of new thinking in this area when it removed its veto of the EU-Turkish customs union in exchange for the European Council of Ministers's commitment to accelerate membership negotiations with Cyprus. Turkey wishes to become "European" and Greece has every reason to favor it. In searching for additional tradeoffs that would benefit both countries, Greece can begin a process of stabilizing its relations with Turkey that is long overdue. Greece, no less than Turkey, needs to look west. That is where the future of Greek security will be determined.

Developing policies to achieve greater security at less cost and to reduce the incompatibility between Greek foreign and domestic policy will require fresh thinking and a more influential policy-making role for those forces for reform that Nikiforos Diamandouros believes are gaining momentum in Greece.[9] Among the most important questions to be addressed are the following:

Is a stronger European defense identity necessarily in Greece's interest? Since the Western European Union has declared Greek-Turkish differences to be beyond its scope, and the organization's central objective is to enable its members to "protect vital common interests outside Europe,"[10] it appears that WEU membership adds to Greece's military responsibilities without providing security assurances in the area of greatest Greek concern.

Greece's position as a Balkan state prescribes its need for European allies. Its position as a Mediterranean state entails wider defense responsibilities and the need for a strong sea-oriented alliance. Despite Greece's anger over NATO's inaction in Cyprus in 1974, and recent Greek dissatisfaction with NATO's actions against the Bosnian Serbs, isn't it true that membership in the alliance has

---

9.   See P. Nikiforos Diamandouros, "Greek Politics and Society in the 1990s," Chapter 2 in this volume.

10.   The words are those of Assistant Secretary of State for European and Canadian Affairs Richard Holbrooke, "America, a European Power," *Foreign Affairs*, Vol. 74, No. 2 (March/April 1995), pp. 38–51.

generally served Greece's security interests? Although the Greek government has never succeeded in obtaining assurances that NATO's security guarantees would apply in a conflict between two member states, NATO, unlike the WEU, has never declared Greek-Turkish differences to be outside its competence. Furthermore, Greece's defense relationship with the United States is through NATO. If that relationship is allowed to deteriorate, can Greece count on European powers to take up the slack? In terms of its orientation and priorities, the North Atlantic alliance is assuming a more Mediterranean look after the Cold War. The appointment of a Spaniard, Javier Solana, as secretary-general, and France's decision to work more closely with NATO's military wing, suggests the advisability of closer Greek cooperation with NATO than has been the practice since 1974.

In reviewing policies toward Turkey, Greek policymakers have no reason to conjecture that either a Turkish military government or a fundamentalist government would be more favorable to Greek interests than a Turkish government seeking closer ties with the West. Quite the contrary. Why then does it serve Greek interests to impede Turkey's efforts to secure membership in the European Union? Even with active Greek political support, the economic and social problems to be overcome assure that Turkish association will be gradual and slow. Greece's present position simply enables other EU members to hide their own objections behind it.

Greece has an obvious stake in Balkan stability. The Cold War stabilized the Balkans by means of an external balance of power maintained by NATO and the Warsaw Pact. A new, internal balance of power is needed today. As a Balkan and Mediterranean state, and as a member of both NATO and the European Union, Greece is in the best position to provide regional leadership in constructing a Balkan alliance system. Where should it begin? As Misha Glenny suggests,[11] the Bulgarian-Greek relationship may be the logical fulcrum from which to create a new balance of power in the southern Balkans. This, in turn, would strengthen Greece's hand in its dealings with Turkey.

---

11. See Misha Glenny, "The Temptation of Purgatory," Chapter 5 in this volume.

Chapter 5

Misha Glenny

The Temptation
of Purgatory

Momentous changes are being negotiated in the Balkans at present which will have substantial effects on political, economic, and security issues influencing the region. The peace being sought in Croatia and, above all, Bosnia, is by no means merely a way of silencing the guns, although this is a very important part of the deal. The events of the last six months amount to a fundamental restructuring of the unpredictable constitutional arrangements which have characterized the peninsula at regular intervals since the collapse of the Ottoman and Austro-Hungarian empires.

The trigger for this most recent convulsion in the Balkans was the collapse of Soviet power in Eastern Europe, which had an immense influence on the events in Yugoslavia, even though the latter was not integrated into the Soviet Union's structures of political, military, and economic power.

The effects of the Yugoslav crisis and the end of communism in Romania, Bulgaria, and Albania have been far reaching throughout the Balkan peninsula. However, the wars in Slovenia, Croatia, and Bosnia-Herzegovina have obscured the implications of this for the rest of the region.

At the outset, it is important to note that Greece's foreign policy establishment was extremely ill-prepared for the changes in the former communist areas of the Balkans. The postwar settlement in the Balkans meant that Greece's relations with Romania, Bulgaria, and Albania had been reduced to a minimum. It cultivated cultural

---

Misha Glenny is a journalist and writer. He has covered Eastern Europe and the former Yugoslavia for over ten years.

These remarks on events in the Balkans were made in October 1995 [editors' note].

and some economic ties with the former Yugoslavia from the mid-1950s onward, but most of its diplomatic efforts were concentrated on its relationship with Turkey. Yugoslavia developed much stronger economic ties with Germany, Austria, Italy, Czechoslovakia, and Hungary than it did with Greece. Albania's self-imposed isolation ensured that there were no substantial security problems to the northwest, and the Greek-Bulgarian border was one of the most stable along the iron curtain. But Greece, of course, did have a very awkward relationship with Turkey.

As a consequence, there were glaring lacunae in Greece's understanding of what was going on in the northern Balkans when the collapse accelerated from 1989. The crass level of knowledge displayed by some Greek diplomats about the northern Balkans revealed the degree to which this region had been neglected since the war. The converse was not true. All communist countries could boast fairly impressive knowledge of Greece, thanks largely to the bloated intelligence services which were part and parcel of the communist period. Yugoslavia, Albania, Bulgaria, and Romania all maintained extensive information-gathering networks inside Greece, which afforded them a relatively sophisticated understanding of Greek policy.

Greece presented itself rather ostentatiously as the European Community's (EC) representative to the 1988 (Belgrade) and 1990 (Tirana) meetings of Balkan foreign ministers, an embryonic Cooperation Council. This began a period of unsubtle diplomacy in which Greece attempted to portray itself as the godfather of Balkan diplomacy. In the 1990 meeting, Foreign Minister Andonis Samaras expended some effort excluding Italy (which had been granted observer status) from the inner deliberations of these conferences, thus placing a wedge between Athens and its partners in the EC that would later develop into a serious rift. (It is encouraging to note that this rift is now being closed.)

Instead of exploiting the possibilities offered by the opening of the Balkans, Samaras's regime did much to alienate pro-Greek elements, notably in Albania and Macedonia[1], but to an extent in Bulgaria as well. The fundamental assessment that these countries

---

1. The terms *Macedonia* and *Republic of Macedonia* are used as shorthand for the Former Yugoslav Republic of Macedonia (FYROM). Their use does not imply a political position in Greece's dispute with FYROM.

were primarily a security threat to Greece and that Athens should pressure them to concede its goals was an egregious error. Constantine Mitsotakis's removal of Samaras amounted to a recognition of the problems the foreign minister had created, and also marked a serious attempt to rectify them. Since then, with the exception of the single greatest error of Greek foreign policy (Andreas Papandreou's imposition of a total commercial blockade on the Republic of Macedonia in February 1994), Greece has been clawing back the lost ground of the Samaras period and is now in a position to provide one of the most powerful motors for diplomatic reconciliation and economic expansion in the region.

From the point of view of integration with Western structures, Greece is the most influential state in the Balkans. However, instead of exploiting this relative strength to attract the former communist states in the Balkans, Greece behaved in an unnecessarily arrogant fashion toward most of its northern neighbors. Not only did this lead to serious criticism of Greece within the European Union (EU), but it also clearly damaged Greece's own long-term interests in the Balkans. Greece's interpretation of its political influence paradoxically undermined that very influence. It is extremely encouraging how, in the past twelve months in particular, influential circles in Athens (not just in the Foreign Ministry), and equally significantly in Thessaloniki, have recognized the extent of the mistakes made between 1989 and 1994 and are now moving to rectify them. All countries in the region (especially Greece, the Republic of Macedonia, and Albania) are already beginning to reap the diplomatic and political benefits of Greece's more measured policy. Obviously, other states in the region had to make compromises and tone down some of their more hysterical positions, but Greece's greater influence in the region means it carries the greater responsibility.

I must stress that between 1992 and 1994, in the foreign ministries and editorial offices of London, Bonn, and Paris, Greece was being regularly pilloried in the most extreme terms because of its position on the Republic of Macedonia. Given Greece's relative weight in the European Union, this represents a serious diplomatic failure of Athens. This has had the added effect that Greece's constructive role in attempting to solve the conflicts in Croatia and Bosnia has been largely ignored. The governments of both Mitsotakis and Papandreou kept open channels to Belgrade throughout the crisis and provided an important counterweight to the general demonization of Serbia. On occasion, the European Union relied on these friendly relations in order to get messages through to Belgrade. Nonetheless, Greece may take some pride in the knowledge that its persistent support for a negotiated, non-military solution in Bosnia and Croatia has now won general acceptance. Some EU countries have also recognized that the Mitsotakis and Papandreou governments played a significant role in persuading Slobodan Milosevic not to engage in the Bosnian or Croatian conflicts with the full might of the Yugoslav army.

It is imperative that I now deal with the northern Balkans, as this is the laboratory where the most bold political experiments are currently underway. I will conclude with an assessment of what the research in the northern Balkans holds for the slightly less dramatic processes being tested in the southern Balkans.

It is most probable that we are now witnessing the end of the Bosnian conflict, which would be swiftly followed by a compromise solution to the dispute between Serbia and Croatia over eastern Slavonia. The deal being negotiated by Assistant Secretary of State Richard Holbrooke could, of course, break down overnight, but it probably stands a better chance of working than all other attempts to broker a solution hitherto.

However, even if all the principles and territorial division of the new Bosnian state are agreed upon, there will be enormous difficulties implementing this arrangement. The reason for this is not because all Bosnian citizens are wild, Balkan peoples intent on revenge, as the old cliché would have us believe. It is simply that the peace agreement being improvised at each meeting of the three foreign ministers of Croatia, Bosnia, and the Federal Republic of Yugoslavia amounts to a unique and novel constitutional construct in Europe's modern history.

Significantly, Holbrooke is not using any constitutional lawyers to help draw up these documents. This may go some way toward explaining why there are so many inherent contradictions in the constitutional base of the new Bosnian state, as enshrined in the two agreements of September 8 and 26, 1995. They amount to nothing more than diplomatic improvisation, although it is impor-tant to stress that this in no sense implies that they may not work. But the only way the deal is going to work without Bosnia sinking back into the mire of armed conflict is if the Serbs and Croats are able to exercise power decisively in their respective para-states in

Bosnia, however distasteful this may be to the Bosnians or members of the international community.

Until the United States put its weight behind Croatia's war aims in the Serb-held Krajina, the Yugoslav conflict was in a logjam. This was loosened by the Americans' decision to drop their support for the Muslims, based almost exclusively on moral criteria, and shift it over to the Croats for purely political reasons.

This change, which has evolved over the last fourteen months, saw the United States move closer to the German position on Yugoslavia and away from Great Britain and France. The diplomatic and military support for Croatia from Bonn and Washington was simply too powerful for London and Paris to resist. When the Croats decided to solve the Krajina question by military means and cleanse it of its Serb population, they did so with the tacit support of the international community.

This represents the real turning point in the Yugoslav wars. As the Americans correctly argue, the emergence of a strong Croatia alters the regional balance of power and does enable a peaceful solution. But it is a solution that prefers ethnically pure states over states with a mixed population. After the Krajina has been cleared and Croatia has established itself as a powerful and confident military power, Bosnia will be divided.

As a consequence, the Yugoslav idea (the coexistence of Serbs, and Croats in Croatia; the coexistence of Muslims, Serbs and Croats in Bosnia) is coming to an end. This is a significant historical moment. In place of Yugoslavia, the international community now supports and encourages two strong nation-states in the northern Balkans to maintain the balance of strategic and political power. Whether this will succeed or not is still a mystery. But this solution to the collapse of Yugoslavia in the northern Balkans does raise a serious political question in the south.

The peoples, or more precisely the political elites, of the southern Balkans have until now decided against entering into armed conflict as a solution to the problems thrown up by the collapse of Yugoslavia. They have had ample opportunity to do so, and occasionally parts of the region have come closer to collapse than may be apparent.

The emergence of the Republic of Macedonia as an independent state may be regarded as a process mirroring the creation of a Bosnian state in the north. Here is a country which is viewed with hostility by its more powerful neighbors; whose territory occupies a key strategic area; whose majority nationality has only recently assumed the characteristics of modern nationhood; and whose short-term or long-term existence is dependent on the continuing goodwill of a large minority population with connections to one or more of the neighboring states.

But despite these similarities between the two feeble state constructs, war has not come to the southern Balkans. I would venture three main reasons for this. First, the conflict in Bosnia itself has had a powerful sobering effect on the Albanians and Macedonians inside the country. The breakup of the Macedonian state would almost certainly result in ferocious bloodshed, and neither nationality is willing to risk this at the moment. Second, the country was not squeezed between two participants involved in an active war in the way that the Serbs and the Croats suffocated the Muslims of Bosnia-Herzegovina. And finally, fighting between Albanians and Macedonians would probably trigger the intervention of the Serbs and possibly the Bulgarians. The Albanians probably do not feel confident enough of their military capability to enter into such hostilities—the local Albanian population has grievances enough against the authorities in Skopje. But the dominant part of its leadership has always worked hard to ward off armed confrontation with the Macedonian police.

But the solution to the northern Balkan question, based on the consolidation of a Greater Croatia and a Greater Serbia, will in time raise the issue of a Greater Albania in the southern Balkans. The northern Balkans has made its decision at the crossroads and is steadily marching down a bloody road off into the unknown. The southern Balkans is still standing at the crossroads. The treaty between Skopje and Athens, signed on September 13, 1995, in New York City, is a desperately needed signal that the various states in the southern Balkans are going to think very hard before running down the road of confrontation, regardless of the grievances between them. While the Skopje/Athens agreement does not solve the fundamental problem of Macedonia's stability, it does give everybody in the region a certain hope that a treaty system may emerge as a powerful disincentive to armed struggle.

It is important to stress that, following the collapse of communism, the southern Balkans may boast, in theory, one of the greatest potentials for economic expansion and swift growth in central and southeastern Europe. Much time has been wasted. The imposition of the commercial blockade on Macedonia by Papandreou in February 1994, was a serious blunder in economic terms for Greece. It is no coincidence or surprise that the industrial and business communities of Thessaloniki were the most vigorous advocates in Athens of a compromise deal with Skopje to lift the blockade. This has compounded the damage caused by the Yugoslav war (and the closing of the transit route through Slovenia, Croatia, and Serbia) to the regional economy. The alarm bells rang more insistently during the past year with the proliferation of disagreements between the Serbian and Greek authorities over commercial issues and facilities at the port in Thessaloniki. In addition to this, the closing of the border has prompted the authorities in Tirana, Skopje, and Sofia to accelerate plans to expand rail and road links, which, if realized, will have a long-term negative impact on Thessaloniki's prospects. The Vergina sun has now, of course, been dropped from the flag. Despite Papandreou's tough remarks about the name on September 1, this is unlikely to cause a problem, as both governments appear happy in private to postpone resolution of the problem and live in a political never-never land.

Now that the border is open, Greek business must move swiftly to claim a dominant position in the Republic of Macedonia's economy, in which Italian, German, and, most prominently, Bulgarian capital has been showing considerable interest.

But Greece has steadily improved its relationship with Bulgaria, and the deepening of commercial ties between Athens and Sofia now look set to pay some dividends, especially in Macedonia and Thrace.

I believe that the emerging relationship between Greece and Bulgaria deserves more attention than it receives. Here are two countries whose relations in the twentieth century have been dogged by nationalist and ideological disputes. Yet, both are moving as fast as possible to anchor their new relationship in economic and commercial ties. Goods are moving; new borders will soon be opening. This not only generates regional growth in the southern Balkans; it also places Greece in an advantageous position when the markets of Ukraine and Russia begin to open up.

The Greek-Bulgarian relationship (although not without its problems) should be used as a model for interstate relations in the southern Balkans. The Bulgarians have also succeeded in improving their relationship with Turkey in this respect, dampening what at one point may have been a dangerous nationalist dispute in the region.

The only way that peace and economic growth can be guaranteed in the southern Balkans is through the establishment of a system of bilateral treaties between states. These treaties could then be used as a base for a multi-layer cooperation organization. Such treaties would have to deal with two fundamental problems: borders and minorities. There is a certain ironic circularity to the complaints that Greece directs against Albania about Tirana's treatment of its Greek minority, that Albania directs toward the Republic of Macedonia about Skopje's treatment of its Albanian minority, and that the Republic of Macedonia directs toward Greece about Athens's treatment of its Slav minority. These questions are best resolved by the parties involved without international interference. If, however, the United States felt that its strategic interests were threatened by such disagreements, it may well apply unpleasant pressure on local governments. This is not desirable in my opinion.

A solution to the Macedonian question, satisfactory to all parties, is the key to stability and growth in the southern Balkans. Whether one is hostile or not to the creation of a Macedonian state, one must realize that the collapse of this state will lead to war. The attempted assassination of President Kiro Gligorov is a sobering reminder just how delicate the political stability of the Republic of Macedonia remains. Greece has responded in the most commendable fashion to the event—offering medical aid to the president and continuing the negotiating process with Skopje in the most discreet and effective manner.

The Republic of Macedonia must be maintained in its present borders (any attempt to change the borders in any direction is a recipe for disaster) to prevent a destabilization of the southern Balkan region and an accentuation of geopolitical tensions drawn roughly along concessional lines. This will entail the government in Skopje making some bold concessions (e.g., over the status of the Albanian minority), but it will also mean a reciprocal demonstration of goodwill from all the country's neighbors.

The disintegration of Yugoslavia has provoked a significant increase in the involvement of more powerful states in the Balkan region. The inability of the European Union to contribute to a stable constitutional settlement in the northern Balkans has led to a growth of American involvement in the region as noted above.

Since the collapse of communism, the United States has taken a much more vigorous interest in the southern Balkans than have most member states of the European Union, despite the fact that Greece is a member of the European Union and Turkey is a perennial applicant. In the immediate aftermath of the revolutions in Bulgaria and Albania, the United States began building close ties with those countries and in particular with their respective presidents, Zhelyu Zhelev and Sali Berisha. The relationship with Bulgaria has cooled somewhat in light of the messy disintegration of the main anticommunist coalition, the Union of Democratic Forces (UDF), although the return to power of the Bulgarian Socialist Party (BSP) has not resulted in any substantial shift in Bulgaria's foreign policy, which remains a force for regional calm. It is also worth noting that the deep mutual affection displayed by both the U.S. State Department and President Berisha in Albania has now cooled considerably.

The United States has also stationed five hundred soldiers in Macedonia within the framework of the UN peacekeeping operation, UNPREDEP. Although Serbia in particular raised strong objections to this deployment of American troops, it is highly unlikely that they would become participants in any possible conflict in the region. They are based at Petrovec airport just outside of Skopje, chiefly in order to ensure their swiftest possible evacuation in the event of any trouble breaking out. They do, however, have an important monitoring function, registering the number and nature of violations of UN sanctions across Macedonia's border with Serbia in addition to a less well advertised intelligence-gathering role.

Twice, the government of Albania has given permission to the United States to station unmanned spy planes in Albania. The latest model, the Predator, is currently monitoring troop and artillery movements in southern Serbia, Bosnia, and Montenegro. During his recent visit to Washington, President Berisha said that he had offered the American military the use of naval and army facilities inside Albania, increasing speculation that the United States is preparing to open a naval base on Sazan island, west of the Albanian port of Vlore.

American interests in the Balkans would appear to be part of a broad strategic plan, albeit one that is rendered confusing by the multitude of different government agencies operating in the area. Generally, the American authorities deny the development of a particular U.S. strategy in the area and, until documentation becomes available, one can only note the intense U.S. diplomatic and military presence in an arc that stretches down from Croatia, across Albania, and into Turkey.

After seemingly having washed its hands of the southern Balkans, the European Union has recently revived its interest in the area. Following painfully difficult negotiations, Greece has now dropped its objections to the creation of a customs union with Turkey, while the European Union at last appears serious about the beginning of negotiations to accept Cyprus as a new member. The agreement between Skopje and Athens will also break the logjam in relations between Brussels and Skopje.

To conclude, I would stress that there are many positive signs in interstate relations in the southern Balkans that hold out the hope that this region will not be seduced into following the suicidal path taken by the Serbs, Croats, and Muslims in the northern Balkans. However, the Bosnian situation still remains a very deep mess. Even if a solution to the conflict is found, Serbia, Croatia, and Bosnia will all have to deal with the shattering problems caused by the massive transfer of populations affected by the war. The numbers of displaced people are comparable to the Great Exchange between Greece and Turkey, with all the attendant difficulties of social and economic integration of populations whose traditions are not suited to their new homes. It is essential for Greece and the other countries in the southern Balkans to pursue better relations through careful and committed negotiations. However, for some time to come, the region is likely to be hostage to the unpredictable events in the north. This is not an especially encouraging situation, but it would be foolish to assume a fatalistic position which considers the Balkans unable to extricate itself from intractable security problems.

What Is to Be Done?

Chapter 6

Dimitris Keridis

Greece in the 1990s:
The Challenge of Reform

Greece is in crisis. Its economy, overburdened by the excesses of the 1980s and the demands of globalization, is in need of painful structural reforms. Such reforms are not possible without a parallel effort to do away with a political culture based on populism and clientelism.

Since independence, scholars have debated about the deeper causes of Greek distress. Some have blamed the Ottomans, some the Bavarians, and others the recent misfortunes that afflicted the country. The debate, far from over, often entertains the metaphysical. It should not be so. One has to look not only to the strong inflation and deficit-free growth of the 1950s and 1960s, but also to the Cypriot economic miracle of the 1970s and 1980s. Cyprus has proved that centuries of Ottoman rule, a Christian-Orthodox heritage, a national tragedy, and a lack of natural resources are no obstacle to a first-class public administration and a dynamic, prosperous economy of full-employment and minimum social inequalities.

Since 1990, Greece has made a determined and quite successful effort to put its public finances in order and restore macroeconomic stability. The budget deficit has come down twelve percentage points, from twenty percent to eight percent of gross domestic product (GDP). To realize the full extent of the progress, one may compare such results with the current debate between the U.S. Congress and the Clinton administration over balancing the U.S. federal budget in seven years, a net gain of less than three percent of the U.S. gross domestic product. Greece has managed to achieve

Dimitris Keridis is Research Associate at the Institute for Foreign Policy Analysis, Cambridge, Massachusetts, and a doctoral candidate in international relations at the Fletcher School of Law and Diplomacy, Tufts University.

one year, and, on average, every year since 1990, what the United States is trying to achieve in seven. Since 1992, the country has run primary surpluses for the first time in decades. If 1993 had not fallen victim to the political cycle of the economy and 1994 to the timidity of PASOK's first year in power, the results of fiscal consolidation and price stabilization could have been even better.

However, public debt is still rising and there is a long way to go before achieving nominal convergence with the rest of the European Union in order to participate in Europe's single-currency project. Far worse, real convergence has been elusive for fifteen consecutive years. The Greek economy has stagnated too much for too long, and there is a growing demand for strong growth that will create new jobs and raise standards of living. Unleashing the growth potential of the Greek economy is not incompatible with stabilization. On the contrary, stabilization "as usual" has reached its limit. It will be a grave mistake if the current euphoria, resulting from growing confidence in the economy and PASOK's compromise with economic rationality, misleads Greece into believing that convergence is possible without reform. With "politics as usual," recent progress might be reversed and Greece will remain a constant underperformer in the European Union.

Greece's stabilization strategy has been based on a tight income policy, higher taxes, and a strong drachma policy. Structural reforms have been minimal and timid. New Democracy did succeed in overhauling the social security system and privatizing some public firms and PASOK did take some measures to combat tax evasion and broaden the tax base, but generally the government has been very reluctant to proceed further in the interests of social peace. Most often, the reformist agenda has been driven by external pressures and the European Union. Greek governments have reacted to change defensively, instead of embracing it wholeheartedly and making the most of it.

If there is a Greek paradox, it should be found in the particular ways the Greek state came into existence and grew up in the last two centuries. An informed analysis of the Greek predicament should begin with a brief summary of some developments that still influence modern Greece:

First, the outbreak of the Greek revolution in 1821, which led to the Ottomans' sudden and forceful withdrawal from the Peloponnese and Roumeli, left behind vast lands in the hands of the Greek state ("national lands"), which were later distributed to farmers. With the exception of Attica and Thessaly, until the land reform of 1917 (fully implemented in the 1920s), Greek farming has been dominated by small, low-productivity plots.[1] The absence of a large agricultural proletariat (wage labor) has saved Greece some of the turmoil that has afflicted other Balkan countries, while the early linkage of Greek peasants with property has been responsible for their political conservatism.

Second, among the sultan's subjects, Greeks were among the very few to develop a class of merchants and administrators who could provide the much-needed capital and skills to run the newly established Kingdom of Greece.[2] However, from the inception of the nation-state, Greek capitalists were reluctant to invest in manufacturing; they preferred trade and financial activities where profit margins were greater.

Thus, the Greek economy has been dominated by services, and often, a variety of parasitic, intermediary activities, and an uncompetitive agricultural sector.[3] This, coupled with the small, family size of most economic establishments and the inefficiency of the state bureaucracy, has given rise to the development of a vast underground and untaxed economy which, on the one hand, supplements personal incomes and sustains consumption but, on the other, competes unfairly with the official economy and deprives the public treasury of important tax revenues.

Third, the strong resistance of local chieftains to centralization, implemented first by Capodistrias and later by the Bavarian Regency, led to a historic compromise: as the state grew, it embraced the patronage networks of local bosses.[4] In exchange for

---

1.   Kostas Vergopoulos, *To Agrotiko Zetema sten Hellada: To Provlemata tes Koinonikes Ensomatoses tes Georgias* (The Agrarian Question in Greece: The Problem of the Social Incorporation of Agriculture) (Athens: Hexantas, 1975), pp. 90–91.

2.   John Anthony Petropoulos, *Politics and Statecraft in the Kingdom of Greece 1833–1843* (Princeton, N.J.: Princeton University Press, 1968), pp. 25–26, 35.

3.   Nicos P. Mouzelis, *Modern Greece: Facets of Underdevelopment* (London: Macmillan Press, 1978), p. 27.

4.   Nicos P. Mouzelis, "Greece in the Twenty-First Century: Institutions and Political Culture," in Dimitri Constas and Theofanis G. Stavrou, eds., *Greece Prepares for the Twenty-First Century* (Washington, D.C.: Woodrow Wilson International Center for

their loyalty to the crown, they acquired influence in the ever-expanding state apparatus. Patronage and clientelism were the price that Greece paid for building a national, centralized state.

Fourth, the above compromise was refined during the reign of George I, but came under attack with the Goudi military revolt of 1909. Much of the political history of Greece since then has been a struggle to open the system of oligarchic parliamentarianism to mass participation and respond to repeated crises of national and social integration (of the new lands in 1912–13, of the refugees in 1922,[5] and of the radicalized underclass after World War II).

Twentieth-century Greek politics have been dominated by cleavages (the National Schism of 1915–17 and the Civil War of 1946–49), charisma (Venizélos, Constantinos, Karamanlis, and the Papandreous), populism, and messianism. Eleuthérios Venizélos brought the ascending bourgeoisie into the system. The Left demanded the same for the urban underprivileged classes some years later.

The process was complicated by the 1922 Asia Minor disaster and the 1941 occupation of the country by Hitler's forces. In 1922, Greece was presented with the formidable task of integrating into the national body 1.5 million newly arrived and destitute refugees from Asia Minor, while the hardships of World War II radicalized vast parts of the Greek population who distanced themselves from the bourgeois politics of the Venizelist republic.[6] The civil war established an exclusivist state of the victorious Right against the vanquished Left. Despite some progress (1963, 1974), the process of national integration was only completed in 1981 with PASOK's electoral landslide, and national reconciliation was firmly consolidated with the June 1989 coalition government of the Right and Left and the November 1989 ecumenical government of all three major parties.

Scholars, 1995), pp. 18–20; and Petropoulos, *Politics and Statecraft in the Kingdom of Greece*, pp. 53–56, 514–515.

5. George Mavrogordatos, *Stillborn Republic: Social Coalitions and Party Strategies in Greece, 1922–1936* (Berkeley, Calif.: University of California Press, 1983).

6. Mark Mazower, *Inside Hitler's Greece: The Experience of Occupation, 1941–44* (New Haven, Conn.: Yale University Press, 1993).

And finally, modern Greece has both benefited and been overburdened by its glorious past. Thanks to classical antiquity, Greece has been able, alone among all Balkan and Christian-Orthodox nations, to invoke a special bond with the West. Sometimes, however, national development suffered from a fruitless effort to revive old glories, as witnessed in the famous debate over the official language of the country. Moreover, despite Greek success in building a prosperous and democratic national society, when judged against the achievements of their ancestors and the advanced West, there is a sentiment of failure and unfulfilled expectations.[7] Greeks react defensively, feeling inferior and superior toward Westerners at the same time, and so complicating their efforts at making an honest assessment of the nation's strengths and weaknesses, successes and failures.

Greek mainstream political ideology has been dominated by the desire to catch up with the advanced West and become part of the First World. The country imported its political institutions from the West (royalty, parliamentarianism, centralization). As is the case in all late-modernizing countries where capitalism, rationalism, and parliamentarianism are a foreign import rather than an indigenous development, Greece has not escaped an often-ferocious debate between elitist advocates of modernization and cultural Westernization and the Hellenocentric, populist advocates of a Greek-Christian Orthodox heritage that should be preserved at all costs.[8] Simplistic as this dichotomy is, it has informed Greek political debates from the time of the Enlightenment, before the creation of the modern Greek state, to the present day.

The modernization debate has been less between the past and the future than between different pasts and different futures. Both political cultures have been able to draw strength from the country's competing historical "pasts": classical antiquity and Byzantium. Although there have been many attempts to achieve a synthesis and a continuum for all the historical engineering required, political leaders have used the antithesis to sharpen their message

---

7. Christos Yannaras, "Opseis Neoellinikou Viou" (Aspects of Modern Greek Life), *To Dentro* (Athens), Summer 1994, pp. 30–32.

8. P. Nikiforos Diamandouros, "Politics and Culture in Postauthoritarian Greece," in R. Clogg, ed., *Greek Politics and Society in the 1990s* (forthcoming), p. 18.

and cement their supporting social alliances. When current Prime Minister Constantine Simitis attacked the Papandreou leadership, he drew support from this rhetoric and presented himself as the competent Eurocrat who could further modernize and Europeanize Greece.

In sum, the Greek economy is characterized by small economic establishments of self-employed workers, the lowest percentage of wage labor in the industrialized world, an unproductive agriculture, a small manufacturing base, and an overinflated service sector. All these factors contribute to the rise of a large underground economy, as well as to an almost permanent fiscal and balance-of-payments crisis.

The royal absolutism and then oligarchic parliamentarianism of nineteenth-century Greek politics, based on the compromise between an expanding, centralizing state and the extensive patronage networks of local notables, fell victim to the desire of the ascending bourgeoisie first and the lower classes later to acquire a political role. Charismatic politics played a crucial role in breaking or defending the old guard's grip on power. Charisma, however, breeds messianism and political cleavages. Such cleavages were reinforced by the dramatic changes Greece witnessed in the 1910s, 1920s, and 1940s. Political stability was seriously undermined by the differences between Old Greece and the New Lands, natives and refugees, communists and nationalists (national-minded *ethniko-frones*). The military took an active role in politics, opening the door to greater mass participation (1909), establishing a republican order (1922), plotting against the royalists (1933, 1935), defending the established order after 1935, and ultimately closing the door to further mass participation in 1967.[9]

In 1974, the Greek Right, led by the reform-minded Constantine Karamanlis, made its historical compromise with republicanism and liberalism. Karamanlis abolished the monarchy, led the military back to the barracks, and established an open, liberal, inclusive democracy. It was just a matter of time before the other side, excluded from government since 1933 (with few breaks in between),

---

9. Samuel P. Huntington, *Political Order in Changing Societies* (New Haven, Conn.: Yale University Press, 1968), pp. 219–229; and S. Victor Papacosma, *The Military in Greek Politics* (Kent, Ohio: Kent State University Press, 1977), pp. 176–189.

came to power. In 1981, the Greek Left, under the charismatic and populist leadership of Andreas Papandreou, took its revenge.

PASOK's tenure in power oversaw the belated political integration of all Greeks into a stable and consolidated republic. PASOK, however, did not change the basic tenets of the compromise upon which modern Greek politics rest: a large state aiming to satisfy the patronage networks.

In Greece, the conventional dichotomy between the state and civil society is weak. There is no strong tradition of liberalism, of society's rights against state intrusions. State and society are interwoven. In fact, the state is seized, hostage to the demands of patrons and clients alike and has to remain large enough to provide employment opportunities and a messy regulatory regime that invites noncompliance.

Under PASOK, the system reached its perfection and eventual demise. A national party organization centralized the patronage networks. The division of spoils was named "social justice." By 1989, explosive public deficits (20 percent of the GDP) and a stagnant economy bankrupted the ideology of statism and favoritism (*rousfeti*). For two centuries, the Greek state expanded and bought the loyalties of its citizens at the price of extensive corruption and cronyism. The system was eventually undermined internally by the excesses of the 1980s and externally by the demands of globalization and increased international competition.

For all the failures and the persistence of historical addictions, the 1990s stand out as a period of a change in course. State monopolies or oligopolies in broadcasting, telecommunications, transportation, education, health, and financial services are breaking down. A shrinking state will enhance the role of the market in the economy and should strengthen civil society.

At the same time, Greek politics have entered a new phase characterized by the end of charismatic politics and polarization, the emergence of ideological convergence and political consensus, the loosening of party discipline, the shortening of political cycles from two terms to one, depoliticization, a growing apathy of the electorate, and a declining interest in politics and parties.

Many politicians and scholars (and usually people who pretend to be both) have criticized recent developments and warned against the end of politics. Things, however, are not that bad. The end of "politics as usual" might signal the growing maturity of Greek democracy and the strengthening of civil society. The withdrawal of

Papandreou, the last of the great charismatic leaders who dominated Greek public life in the twentieth century, and the election of Constantine Simitis to the premiership, was met with a surprising euphoria in large parts of the population who saw Simitis's victory as the end of "Latin American" and the beginning of "European" politics in Greece.

Greece is in need of reform. A few years ago, it was difficult not only to implement but even to talk about reform. Formalism and particularism deflected popular attention away from workable policy proposals and into abstract legalism or personal feuds.[10] Until 1993, PASOK defended a discredited status quo of special privileges and a growing state.

Greece faces both political and economic challenges. The greatest of them all is the quantitative reduction and qualitative change of the state's role in the Greek economy and society. This means two things: free-market reforms and a stronger civil society. The process has already begun, with slow but steady steps forward on both fronts. In fact, reform is precisely what has been happening in Greece for the last ten years. For once, there is now a wide consensus that the state cannot, and should not, try to do everything (and end up doing nothing), but rather limit itself to providing social services and strategic planning (at most) for the economy. This was not the case in 1974, 1981, or even 1985. It took Greece years of economic stagnation and cycles of fiscal and balance-of-payments crises to realize that the *ancien régime* of nationalization, fiscal expansion, tax evasion, and rising deficits has run its course.

A reformist agenda should include the further weakening of the state's productive capacity and the strengthening of its regulatory role in the economy. A return to the basics should mean that the Greek state does at last what states are supposed to do: tax fairly to provide their citizens with a maximum of physical and a minimum of economic security and equal opportunities.

The goal should be the more efficient use of the country's limited resources. The state's bureaucracy should be streamlined, the tax revenues increased without an increase in the tax rates, wasteful public spending cut down, and public investment increased to upgrade Greece's physical and human infrastructure.

---

10. Mouzelis, *Modern Greece*, pp. 134–137; and Mouzelis, *Greece in the Twenty-First Century*, pp. 23–24.

Such an agenda is bound to produce winners and losers. Thousands of public servants and state employees will lose their jobs; tax evaders will have to pay their fair share of taxes; farmers and other social groups will lose billions in state subsidies; and politicians and business will no longer have special access to public contracts and cheap credit. Opposition to change is concentrated in the less-dynamic strata of Greek society. It is concrete, vocal, and thus, politically powerful. On the contrary, support for change is diffused and rendered politically weak because its benefits are spread to the population at large. However, reform will proceed amidst hard choices, electoral take-overs, gains and losses.

Powerful pressures in support of reform, building up for years, are making reform politically feasible and economically unavoidable:

1. Greece, just like any other state, is facing increased international competition selling its goods and services and attracting foreign investment. Economic reform will increase the competitiveness of Greek products, attract inward investment, and lower the costs of servicing the public debt.

2. Greek governments are hostage to the country's large public debt. As sensitive as they are to voters' support, they have to muster the bondholders' trust so that the deficit is financed at the lowest possible cost. Any deviation from orthodox economics and the current reformist agenda will likely shatter the markets' confidence and produce a capital flight that would devalue the drachma, boost inflation, and leave government bonds unsold and the public treasury bankrupt. With the explosion of public debt, Greek politics have become a balancing act between the demands of voters and the confidence of bondholders. Moreover, because most bondholders are voters themselves, they have a stake in the success of reform in their former capacity, although they might not in their latter. Take, for instance, a tax-evading professional who has invested his savings in government bonds: there comes a time when he is willing to pay some extra taxes to make sure his bonds are paid in a proper and timely fashion.

3. For people on credit, the choice is even clearer. They are interested in lower interest rates. They have been a prime victim of the government's tight money policy, and they have only recently begun to enjoy the benefits of lower rates. Under the old regime, this group of people was limited to a few entrepreneurs. Today, however, with the expansion of consumer credit, more and more Greeks borrow money to buy consumer goods and houses. The

more they do so, the more politically damaging would be a sudden increase in real interest rates, which will be the immediate price to pay if markets lose faith in the government's reformist credentials.

4. The success of reform will determine Greece's place in the United Europe. Maastricht accepted the principle of variable geometry. Greece has to prove that it has both the will and the ability to participate in the hard core of the future Europe. The former is not in doubt: Greece wants a strong political Europe to maximize its national security. Its capability, however, remains in question. All mainstream political parties are committed Euro-federalists. There is the widespread feeling that reform is linked with Greece's place in the world and its external security. It is understood that domestic success is essential for strengthening the country's international position and for securing its borders.

5. Ultimately, what necessitates reform is the failure of the *ancien régime*. Between 1972 and 1990, Greece followed an independent monetary policy with the disastrous results of high inflation and low growth. Low growth increased unemployment and social inequalities. Labor's gains during PASOK's first term were more than lost with the policies of austerity after 1985. The 1989–90 fiscal crisis had a sobering effect on the country's electorate and leadership and made clear that the costs of pursuing the discredited policies of the past are much higher than a change of course.

The economics of stabilization and market reforms have traditionally been the exclusive ideological domain of the Center-Right, although there is no absence of dirigist voices in the New Democracy party. The politics of civil society, however, is *par excellence* the domain where a reformed Left could thrive. Neoliberals have shown a complete disregard and lack of appreciation for this other side of reform. They have failed to realize that rolling the state back is not about numbers and balancing the budget but about changing Greece's political system for good. The success of economic reforms is based on a political revolution that will cut the umbilical cord of clientelism between state and society to create a public domain of autonomous social collectivities independent from the state. The neoliberals' failure to articulate, much less to implement, such a vision for the revitalization of civil society has hurt reform and weakened its political appeal. Only when reform is linked with the broader vision of deepening democracy will etatism lose its ideological base and be seriously undermined. Otherwise, there is the danger that petty clientelism is replaced by a grand clientelism, where politicians trade favors with media and private interests for money in exchange for political influence. Correcting the results of state paternalism should not mean the colonization of society by an unregulated market economy.[11] A reformist agenda cannot but include the further democratization of Greece's liberal democracy.

Civil society is not created by administrative degrees and government actions. It springs out of social demands and initiatives. Politicians and scholars can draft constitutions, but civil society is not created from the top down but from the bottom up. It is the product of centuries-old, accumulated social capital. However, there is plenty of room for policy proposals and political reforms that would facilitate the process:

- There is a need for genuine decentralization that would replace the present-day parastate of mayors and governors (*nomarhes*) with responsible, accountable, and fiscally independent local authorities with decision-making power.
- Accountability, hierarchy, and meritocracy in public administration should be encouraged. A national entry examination might provide a merit-based system of selection. The aim is to create a body of civil servants with the knowledge, self-respect, incentive, and efficiency that Greek leftists so much admire in French *fonctionnaries*.
- Certain institutions should increase their independence and accountability, including the judiciary, the central bank, the universities, public utilities, and state enterprises. When not self-governing, the Parliament should select its leadership with a two-thirds majority to provide for maximum consensus and avoid the appointment of party lackeys.
- There should be a separation of Church and state, and a strengthening of the civic dimensions of Greek citizenship. It has been said that Greeks are good patriots but bad citizens. Unless they become good citizens of a rule-of-law state, with rights and duties and a loyalty based on shared principles rather than on shared blood, Greeks will continue to fight for the nation's "rights," while evading taxes and dodging the military draft on a massive scale.

---

11. Jean L. Cohen and Andrew Arato, *Civil Society and Political Theory* (Cambridge, Mass.: MIT Press, 1992), p. 26.

The end of the Cold War, the acceleration of European integration, the problems of the post-1974 heritage, and the arrival of a new generation of leaders in power have forced Greece to reexamine its place in the world and respond to the challenges presented by the state's crisis and the new international order. Greece has the strength to fulfill its potential. If the country does not fall victim to an external crisis, especially with Turkey, that brings to the fore its insecurity and defensive reflexes, the bipartisan reformist agenda has a good chance of success.

Chapter 7

Basilios E. Tsingos

Greece between Yesterday and Tomorrow

At the beginning of *The Great Gatsby*, the narrator informs his reader of the following instruction he received from his father as a youth. "Whenever you feel like criticizing anyone," he was taught, "just remember that all the people in this world haven't had the advantages that you've had." Nick Carraway's childhood lesson seems a particularly apt caution for a book that seeks to explore the economic, diplomatic, and political underperformance of a nation.

But given that we are who we are—that we have received what we have received—what are we to do? The fascinating figure of Odysseus from Homeric epic shows us that success is not so much a matter of being dealt the best hand in life as making the most of the hand one is dealt. Neither the strongest, nor the fastest—and certainly not the "best"—of the Achaeans, Odysseus is, nevertheless, the most resourceful. He is Odysseus *polytropos*, the many-wayed Odysseus. It is his characteristic resourcefulness and resiliency in the face of adversity that ultimately allows Odysseus to survive the horrors of battle and the tribulations of the return voyage and once again see wife and home—unlike many other warriors "better" than he.

Modern Greece, I would venture to say, has much to learn from this forefather as it goes about answering the question "What is to be done?" That Greece faces numerous internal and external confining conditions is incontrovertible, though observers might differ somewhat as to the exact number and magnitude of these constraints. Equally incontrovertible is the suboptimal performance of Greece's economy, foreign policy, and political leadership. This widely shared picture of Greece is one that the contributing papers of this book corroborate and bring into sharper focus.

Basilios E. Tsingos is Lecturer on Social Studies at Harvard University.

But it is all too easy to lay the blame for less-than-ideal "outputs" on less-than-ideal "inputs." In the context of modern Greece, such assignment of blame popularly takes the form of quasi-conspiratorial or neocolonial arguments that emphasize Greece's geostrategic location, or peripheral status, or else it takes the form of an almost fatalistic exploration of aspects of the Ottoman legacy in the economy, state, and society. The problem with such approaches is that they too easily draw one away from the matter at hand: the all-important question, "What is to be done?"

So, what is to be done? Assuming that the "inputs" of the system are more or less constant, how do you increase Greek "performance?" As in auto racing, the answer clearly lies under the hood and behind the wheel. This insight suggests one "meta-answer" and several more concrete answers to our question.

The first step, I would argue, is to realize that the relevant question for Greece (as for Odysseus) is "What is to be done *given that things are the way they are?*" Phrasing the question in this way would entail a shift away from an "entitlement" attitude that, it seems to me, is prevalent in both elite and popular circles in Greece. This is an attitude that tends to focus one's attention and energy on the (I would argue) less-than-fruitful task of what Greece and Greeks deserve (for historical, cultural, moral, or international-legal reasons), rather than what they should do now, given that they have been short-shrifted (as is widely perceived) at some point or points in the past.

To be sure, a call for such an attitudinal shift may seem a rather inchoate proposal that underdetermines concrete answers to the policy issues inherent in the question, "What is to be done?" Nevertheless, it is a profitable meta-answer to this more practical question to the extent that it suggests the direction in which both elite and mass political culture would need to mature in order to facilitate the recognition and implementation of desirable changes.

And what are desirable changes? They are those that help overcome the sociopolitical, socioeconomic, diplomatic, and strategic challenges that threaten future Greek prosperity and security—challenges that are respectively well analyzed in the papers presented by Nikiforos Diamandouros, Stavros Thomadakis, Misha Glenny, and Monteagle Stearns. In what follows, I offer a brief, nonexhaustive, and eclectic list of five such changes or reforms that can partially serve to answer the question, "What is to be done?" Because my own particular training is in international relations, political sociology, and law, I shall strive to limit my comments to those fields.

First, I would venture to say something counterintuitive as far as Greek foreign policy is concerned. Despite the fact that Greece's most pressing security threats lie to its east and north, I would counsel Greece to turn the direction of its foreign policy west. By this I mean Greece needs to adopt a farsighted, "team player" diplomatic strategy and take a more active role in "non-Greek issues"—especially in the area of European integration. Bilaterally, Greece would be well advised to support its allies in *their* time of need in ways that go above and beyond the call of minimum propriety. Things like Greece's infamous response to the Falklands crisis or the Korean Air Lines 007 shoot-down do not die easily in Western diplomatic circles.

There are implications from such observations. Most importantly, Greece sorely needs to concentrate on building up a reserve of diplomatic capital so that it has chips it can cash in during times of real need. Unfortunately, I would not characterize Greek foreign policy at present as one that is directed toward building up a passbook savings account of diplomatic capital. Rather, Greek policy seems ineffective and myopic to the extent that it is predicated largely upon the idea of capital-to-capital shuttle diplomacy in time of need. The results, I think, speak for themselves. Diplomatic panhandling is no more a way to long-term prosperity and security for a nation than panhandling is a viable strategy of financial planning for individuals.

Second, Greece needs to shift more of its language in the international arena away from that of Greek rights and entitlements toward that of Greek interests. Lest I be misunderstood, the reason for such a shift is not that Greece is not in the right under strictures of international law. Almost invariably, I think the facts demonstrate that it is. The problem is that Greece needs to articulate an interest-based reason as well as a rights-based reason for why, say, pressure needs to be put on FYROM or Turkey on issue A or B. To be more effective, Greek appeals to world opinion need to be explicitly (and I would argue primarily) pitched in terms like "regional stability and peace would be facilitated by FYROM or Turkey doing such-and-such, because of X, Y, Z considerations."

To be frank, elite or mass opinion in the West could care less about who in the Balkans can stake the stronger claim to be the true progeny of Alexander the Great. Similarly, the International

Olympic Committee was not overly interested in whether the Olympic Games originated in Greece or even whether Greece "deserved" or was "entitled to" the 1996 Centennial Games. When it got down to brass tacks, as a rough and brash American might say, what mattered was whether Greece was up to the task and was the best of all available places to host the Games. The sooner Greek policymakers and opinion leaders figure out things like this, the sooner their efforts will yield results. Arguments intended for internal consumption and those intended for export cannot be the same, because they have different purposes and different audiences.

This leads to a third suggestion, which could be summarized as taking a page out of the Turkish playbook. I will explain what I mean by this by referring to Samuel Huntington's seminal and controversial argument about civilizational clashes. Whether it is ultimately right or wrong, Huntington's work strongly suggests that the high premium that Greece has put on cultural and historical arguments in trying to sway world opinion on any number of recent issues seems to have been a suboptimal strategy. Either these arguments were vain and superfluous (because Huntington is wrong and culture does not matter) or the arguments failed to resonate because Huntington is right and Greece—together with Serbia, Russia, and the non-Latin Christian East—is on the wrong side of the cultural divide, at least so far as the West is concerned.

But how is this latter alternative possible, one may wonder. Isn't Greece, after all, the birthplace of Western civilization, the crucible in which the Enlightenment values of the contemporary West were forged centuries ago? This is no doubt largely true, but one has to recognize a disjunction between ancient Greek history and modern Greek history, the latter of which, I think it safe to say, most in the West know next to nothing about.

Greece needs to recognize that it cannot move Western or world public opinion by calling attention to its "story" when that story is (as far as modern Greece is concerned) largely unknown, or (as far as ancient Greece is concerned) increasingly forgotten or deemed irrelevant. Nor can you hope to teach such a story in the confines of a press conference. To the extent that Greece wants to tap into a reservoir of positive feelings and empathy for its plight, steps must be taken to communicate the pains and woes of modern Greek history to non-Greeks outside of Greece *on a cultural level*.

There are two key strategies Greece could pursue toward this end. The first would be to take what I term a page out of the "new"

Turkish playbook. At various elite universities in the United States and elsewhere, the Turkish government has recently made substantial and well-publicized gifts to endow the study of Ottoman Turkish culture and history. While one might argue about the merits and demerits of accepting such gifts from the universities' perspective, it seems clear that one could hardly imagine more long-term bang for Turkey's buck. The Greek government and Greek diaspora groups would do well to observe and learn from Turkey's example in this area.

A second strategy for Greece would be to recognize and focus more of its efforts on the power of images and visual narratives in late twentieth century society. More specifically, money of the Greek government and diaspora would be very well spent on funding a Greek *Schindler's List*, in English, about the tragic events in Smyrna in 1922. An alternative project would be a film for popular release about the human story behind the "Kristallnacht" that occurred in Constantinople in 1955. If one can have a major motion picture about Jefferson in Paris, why not one about Byron in Greece?

Fourth, Greece needs to reform its electoral system away from the modified system of proportional representation that is in place today toward a more first-past-the-post system. The desirability of such change flows from the need to ensure stronger, more robust governments in Athens. A common complaint heard about the Greek political class is that its members "know what to do but do not do it." As best as I can perceive, the main reason for this observed dissonance (note the qualification) is not a lack of political will, but rather a lack of political capability.

Recent Greek governments, especially that of Constantine Mitsotakis, are virtually textbook examples of the extent to which precariously perched governments are often hampered in their ability either to commit publicly to a privately preferred policy objective, or else to implement it, because of the ability of intragovernment dissent groups to threaten or to use a "spoiling power" or veto out of all proportion to their strength. As John Major's travails with the Eurosceptics of the British Conservative Party make clear, a first-past-the-post system is not a panacea in this area. Nonetheless, a change in the electoral system is one way to do the tinkering alluded to above so as to improve Greek government performance, especially in the crucial area of decision-making capacity. If those behind the wheel are to drive effectively, the ability of backseat drivers to get their hands on the wheel has to be sharply curtailed.

Finally, the best hope for improved Greek economic performance should be seen to rest in private initiatives rather than centralized governmental efforts. To this end, Greece is in need of various institutional and legal reforms to provide an accommodating framework within which Greek enterprise can operate more efficiently by lengthening what is known in corporate finance as the shadow of the future. It is all too easy to focus on the importance of confidence-building measures in international relations and ignore their crucial necessity as far as business investment, legal infrastructure, and national economies are concerned. The reduction of administrative arbitrariness, political favoritism, *rousfeti*, and a greater implementation of a neutral rule of law, in the truest meaning of that term, would go a long way toward providing the type of springboard necessary for future Greek economic prosperity and social cohesion. To this end, performance-oriented reform and innovation are needed in many areas of Greek law and law enforcement, ranging from the payments system, secured transactions, and bankruptcy, to administrative law and procedure, taxation, and the institution of judicial review.

In conclusion, "What is to be done?" is a question that conveys both the normative query of what *should* be done and the descriptive question of what *will* be done. One can reasonably entertain the idea that the exchange of viewpoints through papers such as those in this book will help to make the future convergence of promise and performance—what should be and what is—somewhat more likely.

Chapter 8

Alexis Papahelas

Greece:
An Agenda for Reform

The domestic and foreign challenges facing Greece in the 1990s require both innovative problem solving and a "can do" attitude to replace the deep-seated cynicism and inertia infecting Greek society today. The time for reformist initiatives has arrived.

The lack of vision and forward-looking leadership in Greece has become apparent as Greek political structures in the 1990s have proven ineffective, even incompetent. The public has lost confidence in the state's ability to handle the country's problems. Recent polls indicate that the main institutional pillars of Greek society are undergoing a serious crisis of credibility and functionality. Political parties, the media, the judiciary and, lately, the armed forces are viewed by the public with skepticism and distrust.

The causes of the failure of these institutions have long been identified and the symposium reexamined them in detail. The task before us now is to move beyond diagnosis and answer the question, What is to be done? Solutions to problems facing Greece must be advanced, I believe, by those people from within Greek society and from the Greek diaspora who are able to look beyond short-term interests because they operate outside the sphere of partisan and business concerns that permeate most debates on issues affecting Greek society. As one means of harnessing that potential resource, I propose the creation of an independent foundation to study the future of Hellenism, an institution that would bring together "wise men" as well as experts from all fields to begin this problem-solving dialogue. As a forum of the best Greek intellectuals, businesspersons, scientists, and artists, discussions might address such challenges as the need for educational reform, Greece's strategic outlook on Turkey, the agenda and priorities for important

Alexis Papahelas is U.S. correspondent for MEGA Television Channel in Greece and Washington correspondent for the BBC World Service.

reforms to be addressed, or the development of foreign policy strategies. Outcomes might include recommendations for short- and long-term action. Funded exclusively by nongovernmental entities, and therefore beholden to no political interest, this forum could potentially become an influential body in Greek political and social life.

One potential benefit of the establishment of a Hellenic foundation would be its role in cementing the bonds of the diaspora's elite with modern Greece. At this point, members of the Greek diaspora are only occasionally called upon for advice, which is often ignored, and they subsequently lose interest in Greek affairs. The Greek diaspora has traditionally played an important role in the creation of the charitable and arts foundations of civil societies around the world. By capitalizing on this energy and actively mining the intellectual and experiential capital of the diaspora's elite, Greece can only profit. Although there is no proof that a foundation could effectively help to meet Greece's new challenges of the 1990s and the millennium, at a minimum it could become a forum for some serious discussions and a vehicle for promoting modernizing initiatives.

The decision-making process in Greek foreign policy is another area of symposium discussion that raises the question, What is to be done? Misha Glenny criticized the Greek foreign policy and intelligence apparatus that has not been properly equipped to deal with the post–Cold War realities in the Balkans. An even more serious problem, I believe, lies in the complete micropoliticization of foreign policy making. The fiasco in the handling of Greece's relations with FYROM proved the need for a foreign policy establishment capable of sandbagging those political leaders who often make important decisions based on instinct and pure political motives rather than facts and agreed-upon policy goals. Greece needs to develop a variety of nongovernmental foreign policy institutions—think tanks, journals, discussion groups—influential enough to inject a dash of realism and strategic calculation into foreign policy debates. Independent funding would be a key prerequisite for independent thinking from these institutions, for part of the current foreign policy establishment depends on state support to an extent that does not allow for questioning stereotypes or challenges to traditional strategic axioms.

This effort to develop alternative means of adding information and ideas into the political system of Greece will require the support of the private sector if these groups are to become truly independent and vocal. The symposium discussion made apparent to some participants that a gap in understanding exists between decision makers and opinion makers in Greece and their counterparts in the United States and Europe. The lack of exposure to and participation in foreign policy debates in venues outside of Greece often lead to surprises and misunderstandings. Some Greek participants, for example, were shocked when American analysts or officials explained current U.S. views on the relative strategic importance of Greece and Turkey.

Regular exchanges between foreign and Greek politicians, media personalities, and foreign policy experts could help narrow the gap and define Greek interests within a more realistic set of parameters. At the same time, a continuous, institutionalized dialogue between them would also make Greece's security concerns more clear to European and U.S. foreign policy elites.

The modernization of the Greek foreign policy and intelligence apparatus needs urgent attention. The inept handling of the recent Imia crisis in the Aegean underscored the weaknesses of Greek decision-making structures. Intelligence gathering and analysis were either flawed or information reached decision makers only after serious delays. At the institutional level, coordination between the Defense Ministry, the Foreign Ministry, and the Prime Minister's office is very problematic. The Greek government should obtain technical assistance and establish mechanisms to handle these contingencies. The modernization and streamlining of these structures is essential if Greece is to move away from the decision-making paradigm of the last fifteen years in which foreign and defense policies were often made by the prime minister without proper deliberation, contingency planning, or implementation strategies. Major foreign policy decisions, like the high-level summit between Prime Ministers Andreas Papandreou and Turgut Özal in Davos in 1988 or the imposition of an economic embargo of FYROM in 1994, were made with minimum input from either the diplomatic or the academic establishment.

Nikiforos Diamandouros touched upon another area for problem solving when he discussed the regime of media ownership in Greece and its implications. The nexus of business interests controlling public procurement and public works, the media organizations, and the financing of political parties and their candidates have all been identified as important forces shaping Greek society. The accumulation of power by small groups of individuals has become controversial in recent times and prominent politicians, like former Prime Minister Constantine Mitsotakis or Speaker of the Parliament Apostolos Kaklamanis, have articulated the need for serious reforms. It is doubtful that any of the established political parties can find the will to proceed with institutional reforms and safeguards that might impose some checks on the concentration and use of power by these groups of individuals. Indeed, some of these problems are universal in nature, since they occur in other European countries as well and have led to unsuccessful reformist efforts—in Italy, for example. But Greece has reached a point where the excessive accumulation of power and influence has become an obstacle to the country's modernization and a barrier to the entry of "fresh blood" into the political arena, and something must be done.

Increased transparency in the procurement process and the enforcement of the regulatory rules already in place can be important first steps. Changes in the financing administration of political parties and their candidates' campaigns are also essential. An increased use of public funds for campaign financing could potentially ease dependency on private funds, which are currently uncontrolled by any rules of transparency or accountability.

Chapter 9

F. Stephen Larrabee

Greece & the Balkans: Implications for Policy

This is a time of great opportunity for Greece in the Balkans. As the chapters by Monteagle Stearns and Misha Glenny in this volume demonstrate, Greece's geostrategic position is not an easy one to manage. But if there is a Greek paradox in this realm, it may be that Greece has not yet lived up more fully to its potential as a leader in the region. In this light, I would like to focus on five issues: (1) Greek reaction to the collapse of Yugoslavia; (2) recent signs of change in Greek policy; (3) Greek relations with Macedonia (FYROM);[1] (4) Greek relations with Turkey; and (5) U.S. policy on Greece.

Greece & the Disintegration of Yugoslavia

Like many countries, Greece was caught unprepared by the collapse of Yugoslavia and the turmoil that it unleashed. The disintegration of Yugoslavia shattered the foundations of Greek policy in the Balkans, and had three important consequences: the emergence of an independent Macedonian state with possible territorial claims against Greece; the opening of prospects for Turkish penetration into the Balkans; and the possibility of the emergence of a Greater Albania. In short, the disintegration of Yugoslavia threatened to undo Greece's efforts over the previous fifteen years to create a stable security environment in the Balkans.

As Misha Glenny suggests, Greece overreacted to these developments and the resulting policy, especially during the tenure of

---

F. Stephen Larrabee is a senior staff member at RAND in Santa Monica, California.

1. Macedonia is used as shorthand for the Former Federal Republic of Macedonia (FYROM). Its use does not imply a political position in Greece's dispute with FYROM.

Andonios Samaras as foreign minister, was short-sighted and counterproductive. It was driven primarily by internal factors—particularly Samaras's political ambitions and desire to enhance his own political stature—and it resulted in Greece's diplomatic isolation, both in Europe and in the Balkans. Constantine Mitsotakis's dismissal of Samaras represented a recognition of the damage of Samaras's policy to broader Greek interests, especially to relations with the European Union (EU). Even though Mitsotakis sacked Samaras, he continued to pursue essentially the same policies. However, Mitsotakis's room for maneuvering was strongly constrained by his razor-thin majority in Parliament. Had he gained a larger majority, he almost certainly would have pursued a more conciliatory policy toward FYROM.

Andreas Papandreou intensified problems by imposing an economic blockade on FYROM. This action exacerbated Greece's differences with its European partners. Thus, by the middle of 1994, Greek policy had reached a dead end: Greece's relations with two key Balkan neighbors (Albania and FYROM) were poor, and its relations with Turkey, the European Union, and the United States were strained. What is worse, Greece was tacitly allied with a renegade regime (Serbia) that was perceived throughout the West as the main instigator of the conflict in the Balkans. Hardly an enviable position for a small, exposed Balkan state!

The Winds of Change

There are signs, however, that the nationalist wave characterizing Greek politics from 1991 to 1994 has ebbed. Since the end of 1994, a new, more realistic policy has begun to emerge from Athens. This new pragmatic policy has been reflected in Greece's Balkan policy in particular. Since early 1995, Greece has patched up its differences with Albania, normalized relations with FYROM, and lifted its veto of the customs union agreement with Turkey.

As a result, Greece is now in a position to play the role in the Balkans that it should have played from the beginning—that of stabilizer. Greece could—and, one hopes, will—become point man for the European Union in the Balkans. The country has all the assets to play such a role: economically, Greece is the most prosperous state in the Balkans, and, politically, it is the most stable.

To play this role, however, Greece needs the support of the European Union. It needs to be perceived as a predictable and reliable partner rather than a nuisance. Unfortunately, it will take quite awhile for Greece to repair the harm to its relations with the European Union caused by its previous short-sighted policies. Glenny and I agree that the political class in Greece has failed to sufficiently appreciate the alienation from its EU partners caused by the policies pursued from 1991 to 1994. Today, it is common to hear in the corridors of Brussels the view that admitting Greece into the European Union was a mistake, or that Greece does not share many values and goals with the Union.

As a result, Greece today faces a serious credibility deficit. The sooner this deficit is overcome, the better—for Greece and for the European Union. But closing the credibility gap requires a clear vision of where Greece's real interests and future lie. This, in my view, is with Europe and the West. Greek politicians should abandon any idea of the Serb and/or Russian option alluded to by some participants in the symposium. Flirting with these options will only further erode Greece's credibility in the eyes of its Western partners while gaining it nothing in return.

Macedonia (FYROM)

The internal situation in Macedonia is potentially very explosive, as Glenny points out. If these internal problems are not addressed—particularly the tensions between the Albanian minority and the Macedonian government—Macedonia could become a serious threat to regional stability. Greek policy has not helped matters. The economic embargo imposed by the Papandreou government exacerbated FYROM's internal problems and increased the prospects of an internal explosion. Ironically, Greece would be the country most damaged by such an occurrence. Fortunately, as noted earlier, there are signs that the political class in Greece is beginning to recognize this and to adjust Greek policy toward FYROM. The Interim Agreement, signed between Greece and FYROM in September 1995, is an important step toward the stabilization of bilateral relations and could eventually pave the way for resolution of the name issue. If the name issue can be resolved, Greece has a chance to play a stabilizing role in the Balkans.

Greece would derive clear benefits from a stable, independent Macedonian state, just as Macedonia would profit by good relations with Greece. Greece is the most important economic power in the Balkans and has no territorial aspirations toward Macedonia. Macedonia needs Greece, for Greece can provide Skopje with access to the sea for shipment of its products. Good ties with Greece would also allow Skopje to reduce its economic dependence on Serbia. Greece should use its economic potential to draw from Macedonia into a broad network of financial and political ties. Over the long run, success in the economic realm could have a moderating effect on Skopje's behavior and could help to defuse current bilateral tensions. The opposite policy—trying to isolate FYROM—is likely to exacerbate internal tensions in the country and drive Skopje into the arms of Serbia. Neither development is in Greece's interest or that of its European partners.

Turkey

Turkey is an important factor in the larger Balkan equation. It is not uncommon in Greece to hear the view that the worse things are for Turkey, the better they are for Greece. I believe this idea to be fundamentally mistaken. If things go badly in Turkey, the whole Balkans, including Greece, will be negatively affected. A more unstable Turkey would be a problem for the West and for Greece, making the resolution of current bilateral disputes in the Aegean harder, not easier. The same is true regarding Cyprus. Greece is far better off having a Europeanized Turkey that is firmly anchored to the West. While such a Turkey might still be problematic from the Greek point of view, it would pose far fewer problems than an unstable, highly nationalistic, or strongly Islamic Turkey.

In certain ways, Turkey presents the same type of problem as Russia. Is the West better off with an unstable, collapsing Russia, or a stable, democratizing, Europeanized Russia? In my view, the answer is clearly the latter. In the same way, a democratic, Europeanized Turkey is more likely to be an effective partner over the long run than a weak, unstable Turkey.

We cannot just say—as some participants have suggested—that Turkey should be left alone to handle its own problems. The geopolitical consequences of instability in Turkey or Turkey's collapse would be too dire. The West needs a proactive policy that is designed to affect Turkish policy and behavior. The key problem is the lack of a stable government in Ankara. Today, there is no internal consensus on many of the most pressing issues facing the country. The current instability and governmental weakness have strengthened the hand of the military, which, under former prime minister Tansu Ciller, were given virtual free hand to determine policy on the Kurdish issue. It is no accident that the most hopeful period in Greek-Turkish relations—the short-lived thaw after the Davos meeting between Turgut Özal and Andreas Papandreou in early 1988—took place when both countries had strong national leaders, and that those promising efforts at reconciliation eventually collapsed when the domestic position of both leaders began to erode.

In short, strong political leadership in both Ankara and Athens is a prerequisite for a resolution of outstanding bilateral differences. Unfortunately, there is little sign of such leadership today, particularly in Ankara.

U.S. Policy

U.S. leadership, as we have seen recently in Bosnia, remains critical to an overall stabilization of the Balkans. But active U.S. diplomatic engagement has not been limited to Bosnia. The United States has also played an important behind-the-scenes role in facilitating the recent rapprochement between Greece and Albania, and between Greece and FYROM.

In the wake of the Dayton peace accord, the United States may launch a renewed effort to resolve the Cyprus issue. Progress on this issue is key to a broader settlement of Greek-Turkish differences over the Aegean. I disagree with those who advocate solving the Aegean issues first. I believe that movement on the Aegean issues is unlikely without prior progress on Cyprus.

Resolving the Cyprus issue will not be easy—especially in the aftermath of the tensions over Imia—but there are reasons to believe that a new initiative might bear fruit. The first is the more pragmatic Greek policy that has emerged lately. The second is the European Union's decision to open accession negotiations with Cyprus within six months after the conclusion of the EU Intergovernmental Conference (IGC) which began in March 1996. This adds a new dynamic element to the Cyprus equation and could eventually induce the Turkish Cypriot leadership to take a more accommo-dating position. Third, the United States is better positioned today than it has been in decades to play a mediating role.

In the Aegean, confidence-building measures could play a useful role in reducing tensions between the two countries. The Bulgarian-Turkish and U.S.-Soviet experiences may be relevant in this regard. In both cases, confidence-building measures to defuse threat perceptions and to create a better psychological atmosphere facilitated the eventual resolution of broader security issues. For example, a tradeoff between the demobilization and disbandment of the Turkish Fourth Aegean Army and the demilitarization of the Greek Aegean islands might be possible. Similarly, an open skies agreement, comparable to the one signed between Romania and Hungary in May 1991, could help to reduce tensions and lay the groundwork—as it did in the Romanian-Hungarian case—for a broader improvement of political relations later on. Finally, a direct dialogue on security issues between the Greek and Turkish military should be considered.

Many Greek military officers oppose such a bilateral military-to-military dialogue on the grounds that the Turkish military does not have the same status as the Greek military (i.e., there is less civilian control in Turkey). But any resolution of Greek-Turkish differences will require the support of the Turkish military. Thus, it is impor-tant that the Turkish military be part of the security dialogue—not excluded from it.

None of these suggestions are likely, in and of themselves, to lead to a major breakthrough in Greek-Turkish bilateral relations. Taken together, however, they could have an impact on the overall political-psychological atmosphere and create a more propitious climate for resolving larger bilateral issues.

Chapter 10

Susan L. Woodward

Rethinking Security in the Post-Yugoslav Era

For the third time in this century, developments in the Balkans have set the pattern for international order in the period that followed. The Balkan wars and World War I ended the era of the Eastern empires and replaced them with states founded on the principle of national self-determination (although this principle was not actually realized in much of the region). Following World War II and the civil wars that fascist occupation provoked in Yugoslavia, Greece, and Bulgaria, among others, the principle of containment against the spread of communism from the East led to Europe's military and economic partition, beginning in the Balkans with the Truman Doctrine of 1947. Now, the dissolution of Yugoslavia and the wars for national independence in Slovenia, Croatia, and Bosnia-Herzegovina have seen these principles of national self-determination and containment against the spread of security threats taken to their horrifying extreme of ethnic partition and long-term instability. But this Balkan conflict confronts the major Western powers with the gloomy specter of a world dominated by political disintegration, nationalism, and ethnic war, for which they do not as yet have new ordering principles.

For people in the Balkans, this repetitive pattern strengthens already-strong convictions that territorial and national security must be their preeminent concern and that geostrategic criteria and the interests of foreign powers will continue to define domestic possibilities, and even identities. Greek behavior toward the efforts of Macedonia to gain independence follows naturally from this perspective, as does Greek incredulity at the lack of understanding, even dismissal, on the part of its European allies, of Greek (as well as Serbian) security interests.

Susan L. Woodward is Senior Fellow at the Brookings Institution.

Nevertheless, the causes of these most recent Balkan wars and instability reflect a fundamentally different reality in the region and in Europe. This is a new era, despite the apparent repetition of historical patterns. The real security and national threat to countries today is isolation. Isolation—from trade alliances, major-power governing forums, collective security arrangements, and the community of shared values and culture on which these are said to be based—is the greatest threat to national survival in a world of increasing global interdependence.

The honesty of the discussion at this symposium thus deserves applause, however harsh and insensitive it may first appear, because successful adjustment to these new global circumstances requires a change in perceptions and a realistic confrontation of this new reality. Still in transition, neither Balkan nations nor the Euro-Atlantic allies have yet developed perceptions or behavior fully adjusted to this new order. But, as in the past, the locals will have to make their adjustment first. Self-defensive postures in such an environment not only receive no sympathy, they backfire and are counterproductive.

Lessons of the Yugoslav Conflict

The wars in former Yugoslavia, and the role of Greece in this regional crisis, have already taught several important lessons. The first lesson of the Yugoslav wars is that national security is increasingly an economic issue. Interstate aggression and territorial disputes at the border are ever less significant threats to national and regional security compared with the consequences of internal instability and political disintegration. The origins of such disintegration lie in the declining ability of governments to maintain the conditions necessary for economic growth and full employment, to service foreign debts and attract foreign investment, and to mobilize the revenues and redistribution necessary to assure minimal social services and sustain popular perceptions of equity on which social cohesion and political authority depend.

The consequences of disintegration are particularly threatening to neighbors, for example, swelling numbers of migrants and refugees; far-flung criminal networks trafficking in drugs, arms, and stolen goods; growing acceptance of the right of regional and international organizations to intervene based on a government's record on human rights or the treatment of minorities; and the threat that internal violence will spill over or embolden irredentists and incite a chain of reactive nationalism in neighboring states.

This governmental capacity to manage the economy is insepara-ble in both its positive and negative consequences from participa-tion in the regional and global economy. Geostrategically defined foreign policy grows ever less appropriate; the choice for Greece is no longer between a land or sea,[1] a Balkan or Aegean, orientation. The collapse of socialist Yugoslavia followed the collapse of the international basis of its successful policy during the Cold War to protect national security by diversification, having a foot in all three Cold War blocs (East, West, and nonaligned), while the growing economic pressures to "Westernize" and cut defense budgets and investment were disastrous for its economy and especially for its poorer republics and regions. Although the world is said to be devolving into its separate regions, any move to draw new borders on geopolitical grounds and new spheres of mutually exclusive interests is a serious threat to the viability and stability of the Balkan states.

A second lesson to emerge from the Yugoslav conflict is that policies of exclusion, nonetheless, appear to be winning. The choice of nationalism in the internal quarrel and the successful exit from Yugoslavia of its two richest republics, Slovenia and Croatia, began with claims of nationally defined rights to economic resources (jobs, foreign-exchange earnings, revenues from socially owned enterpris-es, capital assets) and exclusion of claimants on national criteria to prevent further decline in their economic fortunes under severe austerity. What outsiders call "ethnic cleansing" in the war in Bosnia and Herzegovina is a much broader phenomenon that varies only in method, whereby territories and their economic assets are being reserved for members of one nation only. Although the expulsion of Muslims from eastern Bosnia in 1991 and 1992 by radical Bosnian-Serb nationalists has rightly been condemned by the international community, the expulsion of Serbs from Croatia was actually welcomed in some quarters as furthering the prospects for peace. The fall of the Berlin Wall, and, with it, the erosion of the rationale for the Truman Doctrine, has left the entire region of southeastern Europe in a profound state of flux as foreign powers

---

1. See "Greek Security Issues" by Monteagle Stearns, Chapter 4 in this volume.

and neighbors redefine economic spheres of interest along with European security arrangements. But, in contrast to the cry in 1989 for inclusive, incorporating structures to replace the Cold War divide in Europe, theories of exclusion—of "rogue states" in the Balkans, of former socialist countries "not ready" for European membership, and of an "outer" ring in the new "concentric circles" of an enlarging European Union—are gaining currency and acceptability.

A third lesson, learned from observing Croatian success and Serbian failure, is that this new political environment clearly favors some tactics of foreign policy over others. Those who approach national security with a defensive posture that emphasizes military conceptions of security and a strong national defense, with an accompanying large defense budget and defensive rhetoric, have thus lost out to those who choose instead to seek out powerful Western allies using lobbyists, public relations firms, and media-controlled propaganda to build an image as Europeanist Europeans. Although Croatian nationalists already had an advantage in their strategy to win German support for Croatian independence and territorial claims, the Serbian rhetoric claiming self-defense against victimization fell on deaf ears, and Serb threats to realign with Russia backfired. Any such attempt by certain Greek politicians will also backfire; the end of superpower rivalry and the weakness of Russia make that threat hollow. The leverage that geostrategic position once gave to the Balkans has largely vanished, whereas Slovenes and Croats, who laid the groundwork for action first by altering outsiders' perceptions of their goals and position, clearly recognized that circumstances were changing and that success depended not only on seizing the initiative but on a strategy that was future oriented. Throughout the region, it appears, those who strategized an ultimate political goal and pursued it, such as Presidents Milan Kučan of Slovenia and Franjo Tudjman of Croatia, have retained the initiative and succeeded far more than those who pursued a reactive, step-by-step, wait-for-the-political-moment-to-be-ripe policy, such as President Slobodan Milošević of Serbia and two administrations in Greece.

In sum, the lesson of the new Balkan wars is that outside powers and foreign publics have no appreciation for or understanding of the security fears of the Balkan peoples. No amount of complaining by Balkan leaders will overcome this insensitivity. Quite the contrary. The popularity in foreign policy circles of such works as Robert

Kaplan's *Balkan Ghosts*[2] and Samuel Huntington's "The Clash of Civilizations?"[3] does not grow from a twentieth-century version of the eighteenth-century fascination with the Levant, but from a search to justify its opposite—an Orientalist view of the Balkans that seeks distance and may be difficult to reverse. It fits with what appears to be an emergent ideology in this transitional period—a "post-realism"[4]—in which deeply imbedded cultural characteristics are believed to determine human behavior and engender hostility. Whether this ideology will supplant the liberal belief that cooperation and inclusion can prevent war or the realist belief that nations pursue their interests, which are in conflict but need not lead to violence, remains to be seen. But its popularity does give an advantage to those who understand the enormous power to be had through shaping perceptions, particularly through the manipulation of cultural symbols and simple messages in the global mass media. The propaganda wars accompanying the violent dissolution of Yugoslavia created a portrait of the Balkans as obsessed with history, wild, violent, and threatening to the values of Western civilization, an image that will be difficult to erase from people's minds. Just as atrocities perpetrated in the war in Bosnia-Herzegovina have made it difficult to counteract this portrait, so also have the Greek nationalists' hysteria regarding Macedonia and the Greek politicians' persistent preoccupation with Turkey as a hostile threat contributed to an unflattering picture of Greece. It will not take many such examples to erode the Enlightenment view of Greece as the cradle of Western civilization and as a European state in its own right, regardless of momentary disagreements in the European Union, in favor of an alternate portrait of irrational nationalists

---

2. Robert D. Kaplan, *Balkan Ghosts: A Journey through History* (New York: St. Martin's Press, 1993), but see his criticism of those who draw the policy implications from this book that one should stay clear of such irrationality, including non-intervention in the Bosnian war, in "After 'Balkan Ghosts'," *The Weekly Standard*, December 18, 1995, pp. 22–23.

3. Samuel P. Huntington, "The Clash of Civilizations?" *Foreign Affairs*, Vol. 72, No. 3 (Summer 1993), pp. 22–49.

4. I owe this term to my colleague at Brookings Institution, Yahya Sadowski, who is writing about the subject in relation to United States foreign policy.

consumed by their own past and a Balkan country that is not fully European.

Agenda for Action

An agenda for action that follows from these lessons would begin with a fundamental rethinking of the concept of security and the accompanying strategic thinking. Thought and behavior that encourage or justify the partition of the Balkans and the isolation of the southern half should be avoided. And while bilateral agreements for security and cooperation in the region may be the most pragmatic, realistic approach today,[5] such a path to regional stabilization is slow and one that is likely to be overtaken by events originating elsewhere.

The event most likely to have long-term consequences is the current international attempt to bring an end to the wars in Bosnia-Herzegovina and Croatia. The U.S. approach to ending that conflict and the subsequent deployment of a NATO-led, multinational implementation force to Bosnia, a European Union–led reconstruction effort, and a regional arms-control arrangement that will (according to U.S. plans) include Turkish assistance in training and arming a Bosnian (federation) army will likely have long-term consequences for the region. Is the Greek government planning a strategy for its troop deployment, financial participation in reconstruction, and contribution to the conception of these policies? Or will Greece find its influence limited, as it did on December 15–16, 1991, during the European Community meeting to decide whether to recognize Slovenia and Croatia as independent states and dissolve Yugoslavia, to obstruction on elements that affect its immediate national interests? Can Greece turn the American attention to Turkish interests in Bosnia and Macedonia and their wish to follow up the Dayton peace accord on Bosnia with negotiations to end the Cyprus conflict (as then Assistant Secretary of State Richard Holbrooke announced) into an opportunity instead of a threat?

Moreover, the proximate causes and consequences of the Yugoslav wars have raised awareness of the surfeit of conventional

---

5. See the contribution on current trends by Misha Glenny, "The Temptation of Purgatory," Chapter 5 in this volume.

arms in the region and the role in escalating tensions that their availability plays. With attention focused on Bosnia, NATO could pursue unnoticed its program to "cascade" the weapons to Greece and Turkey that had to be discarded after the European agreements on conventional arms reductions; but tensions between the two countries must inevitably draw attention to the need for a regional arms-control regime. If policies to equip and train a Bosnian army hand responsibility largely to Turkey, it is difficult to imagine a positive outcome that does not include more cooperation between Turkey and Greece on these issues.

Whether pressures for weapons reductions and defense cuts come from within the region or from the outside, outsiders have become far more sensitive, as a result of the Yugoslav tensions, to the treatment of minorities as an early warning of conflicts that could explode and spread. Cooperation between European organizations with mandates on human rights, such as the European Union, the Council of Europe, and the Organization for Security and Cooperation in Europe, who recognize the benefit of preemptive action to deal positively with minorities, including transborder minorities, recent immigrants, and refugees, should be near the top of the agenda. Here, too, domestic initiatives and ones involving cooperation within the region are preferred far more than pressures exerted by external forces and their methods of conditionality, sanctions, and isolation.

Signatures on a peace agreement for Bosnia-Herzegovina in November–December 1995, and its accompanying cease-fire, are a step in the right direction but do not, however, prevent war from erupting in the southern Balkans. The consequences of the dissolution of Yugoslavia are far from playing out, as Misha Glenny has correctly warned. Peaceful resolution of this process still requires extraordinary statesmanship and restraint on the part of neighbors as well as the parties directly involved.

Greek insistence on certain conditions for Macedonian independence that denied the Macedonians their very identity (above all, by objecting to their country's name) and thus their right to a state, increased the sense of insecurity and threat of the average citizen. The effect was to push Macedonian public opinion in the opposite direction from compromise. Macedonian moderates became more nationalist, and radicals among Macedonian nationalists and the Albanian population gained popular support and became more assertive. Far more rapid and effective means of resolving the dispute would have involved policies that aimed at creating allies among domestic groups within Macedonia and that recognized the economic sources of security. The embargo made the new state far less stable and its politicians less able to be cooperative. Greek politicians and entrepreneurs who hoped to leverage their country's comparative advantage—Thessaloniki's port and financial center, Greek economic and political stability, and Greek membership in the European Union—into Balkan dominance will have a far tougher time today than in 1992, when Greek finance faced little competition and could have monopolized the situation without substantial investment.

Instead, Greece's economic embargo of Macedonia and delays in its recognition worsened the domestic political and economic conditions in Macedonia. This not only made it more difficult for Macedonian leaders to accept a compromise, but also created a more serious threat to the long-term stability of the region. The embargo undermined so severely both the legal economy and the preconditions for democratic development in Macedonia that the very viability (not just the name) of the country is at stake. And a destabilized Macedonia, after all, can only result in a greater threat to Greek stability, because it would include the enlargement or destabilization of Albania.

The extent of the change needed in strategic thinking and foreign policy formulation is perhaps best illustrated by the pressure exerted by the Greek diaspora in the United States to delay recognition of Macedonia and then to delay, into 1996, sending an ambassador to Skopje. A weak U.S. diplomatic presence in Skopje was clearly not in the best interests of Greece. This raises the difficult question of whether an agenda for action should include debate over the role played by this lobby—a group much like the émigré communities of many other countries whose beliefs and interests were formed by the experiences of their emigration and by American policy in that period (in the case of Greece, the Truman Doctrine and American anticommunist interests in Greece and Turkey) and yet who have, as American citizens with their own entrenched interests and networks, enormous autonomy in defining what they perceive to be in the best interest of their homeland.

But Greeks are not alone in needing such adjustment. The absence of any strategic conception in U.S. or European policy for the future of the Balkans explains the increasing reliance on bilateral relations. But bilateralism cannot stop the escalating spirals of nationalism or lay a basis for regional stability. Bilateral-ism can even be counterproductive when external conditions disrupt the basis for that bilateral alliance, and there is no broader set of institutions to cushion that disruption. This occurred, for example, when mutual recognition of the former Yugoslav republics became a central plank in the U.S. diplomatic approach to ending the war in Bosnia and preventing its spread. Overnight, the basis of the current Greek-U.S. and Greek-Serbian alliances—their mutual understandings on nonrecognition of Macedonia—collapsed. Serbia could no longer defer to Greek interests in Macedonia, Greece had to find an independent approach in its policy toward Bosnia, and U.S. policy toward the region as a whole injected a disturbing rise in levels of uncertainty. Diplomatic activity toward Bosnia continued to be orchestrated by the major powers—the United States, Britain, France, Germany, and Russia—who formed the Contact Group in March 1994 without consulting the frontline states. Local initiatives for multilateral, regional economic or security cooperation among Balkan countries became a way for individual states to compete for special relationships with the United States or to gain access to European Union resources, rather than to stabilize relations and reduce that uncertainty.

The lessons of the Yugoslav crisis also extend beyond the conflict itself. It demonstrated that presentation matters. How concerns are heard by outsiders is more important than how they are meant to be heard. Politicians' rhetoric aimed at their own domestic constitu-ents has repercussions in the international arena, and those countries whose leaders do not think—even cynically—about crafting a public image fare less well than those who do. Thus, for example, the partition of the Balkans, which appears to be the result of the Yugoslav wars, has emboldened those within the European Union who see its enlargement as an opportunity to narrow decision-making power to its core states because Balkan behavior, including Greek rhetoric, has provided an additional justification. To the criterion of differences in economic wealth and development in consigning some states to an outer circle, they now hint at reducing the influence of countries seen as disruptive and unpredictable in their foreign relations.

Above all, the profound transformation in foreign policy thinking and behavior now required is unlikely to occur without domestic changes in policy formulation. While this applies to the United States as well, the lessons of the Yugoslav conflict and the Greek-

Macedonian dispute reveal the woeful need for reasoned public dialogue within Greece, as elsewhere, about foreign policy and national interests. The electronic and print media have fueled nationalist sentiments throughout the Balkan region. Without institutionalized mechanisms to provide contending views and sober analysis, even governments find it difficult to demobilize public emotion and to escape the corners into which they have backed when an opportunity to shift presents itself. Institutions that make public dialogue about major issues of foreign policy a regular occurrence and that provide a counterweight to the immediacy, simplification, and capacity for political manipulation of the mass media are essential, as Eleni Mahaira-Odoni has noted, to calm the escalatory dynamic that results from defensive perceptions, unappreciated grievances, and appeals to public emotions in an environment of enhanced uncertainty and an unsettled future.

Chapter 11

Elizabeth Prodromou

The Perception Paradox of Post–Cold War Security in Greece

One of the most important yet underdeveloped themes common to all of the chapters in this volume concerns the way in which increasingly comprehensive definitions of security in the post–Cold War international order may affect Greece's place within the Euro-American security architecture. Monteagle Stearns astutely has pointed out that any assessment of Greece's strategic options at the end of this millennium must move beyond narrow military factors and incorporate political, economic, and diplomatic elements as well.[1] Similarly, Joseph Nye and Susan Woodward have commented on the importance of perceptions as a determinant of Greece's ability to maximize its security interests within the fluid political, economic, and geostrategic circumstances of the post–Cold War era.[2]

My commentary will develop these observations by considering how the changing nature of security[3] and the shifting international and regional strategic landscape have reshaped Greece's value to and role in the Euro-American alliance structure evolving since the

---

Elizabeth Prodromou is Visiting Lecturer in the Department of Politics at Princeton University and Assistant Professor at the Woodrow Wilson School of Public and International Affairs.

1. See Monteagle Stearns, "Greek Security Issues," Chapter 4 in this volume.

2. See Joseph S. Nye, Jr., "Greece and the Balkans: A Moment of Opportunity," Chapter 13 in this volume; and Susan L. Woodward, "Rethinking Security in the Post-Yugoslav Era," Chapter 10 in this volume.

3. An excellent overview of the evolving debates on the changing nature of security is the piece by Richard H. Ullman, "Redefining Security," *International Security*, Vol. 8, No. 1 (Summer 1983), pp. 129–153. A more general approach is found in Karl P. Magyar, ed., *Global Security Concerns: Anticipating the Twenty-First Century* (Montgomery, Ala.: Air University Press, 1996).

start of the 1990s. I argue that Greece faces a perception paradox in security terms, and that this paradox must be addressed if the country intends to realign its strategic role in accord with its strategic interests in the post–Cold War order. I also claim that the perception paradox of Greek security originates with the ambiguities generated by a reconceptualization by Euro-Atlantic policy elites of Western alliance strategy in terms of the twin concepts of the democratic peace and the civilizational paradigm.

In order to explore the notion of the perception paradox of Greek security, my commentary is divided into three parts. The first part summarizes the centrality of the concepts of the democratic peace and the civilizational paradigm to Euro-Atlantic policy-media-academic discussions about post–Cold War global security. The second identifies the specific features of the perception paradox of Greek security that emerge from the attempt to reconceptualize post–Cold War security by integrating the aforementioned two concepts. The third section concludes with suggestions for how Greek policymakers can redefine the country's security role in order to become the anchor for a regional politics of reconciliation in southeastern Europe as a whole. In this respect, Greece can ensure that the current perception paradox does not become a performance paradox where the country's security interests are concerned.

A Post–Cold War Strategy for the Euro-American Security Space

The end of the Cold War brought a general improvement in the global security environment, given the effective elimination of the reasons for nuclear conflict between NATO and Warsaw Pact forces. Nonetheless, the post-1989 era has been marked by a plethora of conflicts around the globe and, particularly with regard to the regional space of southeastern Europe, has underscored the transformation in the meaning of and policies for ensuring Euro-American security. As part of the Euro-American alliance system and, more specifically, as a critical actor in the southeastern European theater, Greece has been affected directly by the changing global and regional security landscape.

The clearest elements in the still-evolving and, at times, inchoate Euro-Atlantic security strategy (as evidenced by the multiple problems associated with the implementation of the Dayton peace accord) have been the concepts of the democratic peace and the civilizational paradigm. The two concepts have had a nearly parallel life span in policy, academic, and media discourse on post–Cold War security in Europe. A review of some representative quotations from all three domains highlights the importance of these concepts to the development of Euro-American security policy.

In the summer of 1993, Samuel Huntington suggested, in one of the most widely cited articles in recent years, that the post–Cold War security map would be defined by conflicts among civilizations:

> As the ideological division of Europe has disappeared [with the end of the Cold War], the cultural division of Europe between Western Christianity, on the one hand, and Orthodox Christianity ..., on the other, has reemerged. The most significant dividing line in Europe ... may well be the eastern boundary of Western Christianity in the year 1500.... In the Balkans, this line, of course, coincides with the historic boundary between the Hapsburg and Ottoman empires.[4]

A few months later, U.S. President Bill Clinton explained in his State of the Union address that "ultimately the best strategy to insure our [U.S.] security and to build a durable peace is to support the advance of democracy elsewhere."[5]

Although Greek security issues are acknowledged in this volume as partly responsible for the gap between the country's potential and its performance, scant attention has been paid[6] to the security paradox for Greece that has emerged with the comprehensive articulation of the democratic peace and the civilizational paradigm along the three axes of the policy-academic-media triangle on both

---

4. Samuel P. Huntington, "The Clash of Civilizations?" *Foreign Affairs*, Vol. 72, No. 3 (Summer 1993), pp. 29–30.

5. Clinton's State of the Union Message, January 1994, quoted in Ido Oren, "The Subjectivity of the 'Democratic Peace': Changing U.S. Perceptions of Imperial Germany," *International Security*, Vol. 20, No. 20 (Fall 1995), p. 147.

6. For a largely overlooked plea to acknowledge the importance of cultural perceptions in changing definitions of security as they affect Greece's political, economic, and geostrategic status, see Susan L. Woodward, "Rethinking Security in the Post-Yugoslav Era," Chapter 10 in this volume. For an example of the policy prescriptions derivative from the perceptions generated by the integration of the concepts of the democratic peace and civilizational paradigm, see Joseph S. Nye, Jr., "Greece and the Balkans: A Moment of Opportunity," Chapter 13 in this volume.

sides of the Atlantic. However, a brief review of the emergent Euro-American security strategy as it has been constructed across media, policy, and academic lines over the course of this decade suggests a problem best acknowledged—and corrected—by policymakers concerned with Greece's regional and international security interests. I will consider each domain in turn to illustrate this point.

In the policy domain, Anthony Lake, assistant to the president for national security affairs, has identified U.S. security interests with "a strategy of enlargement—enlargement of the world's ... community of democracies."[7] Meanwhile, President Clinton's emphasis on "the NATO alliance ... [as] the anchor of American engagement in Europe and the linchpin of transatlantic security,"[8] in tandem with a security strategy aimed at "enlarging the community of . . . free market and democratic nations,"[9] suggested a Euro-American policy consensus on the centrality of the democratic peace to the post–Cold War global security order.

Clinton's acknowledgement that the democratic peace was not a "crusade ... [but] ... a pragmatic commitment to see freedom take hold where that will help us [the NATO alliance] most"[10] explicitly targeted the new democracies in Central and Eastern Europe as a security priority. Meanwhile, the late François Mitterrand, in his capacity as premier of France, stated that the inability of the European Union to stop the war in the former Yugoslavia was at least partially the result of intractable "ancestral hatreds ... [in the] Tribal Europe [of the Balkans].[11] Former Vice Chancellor Erhard Busek of Austria spoke in similar language when he remarked that "the WEU does not well understand the Orthodox portions of

---

7. Anthony Lake, "From Containment to Enlargement," U.S. Department of State, *Dispatch*, quoted in Henry S. Farber and Joanne Gowa, "Polities and Peace," *International Security*, Vol. 20, No. 2 (Fall 1995), p. 123.

8. William Clinton, *A National Security Strategy of Engagement and Enlargement* (Washington, D.C.: U.S. Government Printing Office, February 1996), p. 37.

9. Clinton, *National Security Strategy*, p. ii.

10. Clinton, *National Security Strategy*, p. 33.

11. See articles in *Le Monde*, July 10, 1992, and March 9, 1993.

Europe,"[12] while former U.S. National Security Advisor Zbigniew Brzezinski suggested an expansion of the borders of the Euro-Atlantic security system to coincide with the borders of "the Petrine Europe of the Holy Roman Empire."[13]

In the academic domain, Huntington's claims that "Western ideas of individualism, ... human rights, equality, [and] democracy ... have little resonance in ... Islamic ... or Orthodox cultures"[14] were echoed in the United States by George Kennan, who explained the problematic democratization of and current conflict in the post–Cold War Balkans as a result of the "salient of non-European civilization"[15] thrust into the region during the long history of Byzantine and Ottoman penetration. In the European academic context, George Schopflin explained that the post-communist "Central European countries (Poland, the Czech lands, Hungary, Slovenia) have a reasonably good chance in the long run of moving towards ... rejoining Europe."[16] In his view, "the enracination of [values that made] these lands part of Western Christianity and ... located Central Europe firmly in association with the West"[17] meant that the southeastern European lands, with an Orthodox and Islamic religious history, would be excluded from the community of market democracies presumably to be incorporated into the Western security architecture.

The media on both sides of the Atlantic have also employed the concepts of the democratic peace and the civilizational paradigm to

---

12. "Central Eastern Europe—Politics of Culture," lecture at the Woodrow Wilson School of Public and International Affairs, Princeton University, February 14, 1996.

13. Zbigniew Brzezinski, "A Plan for Europe," *Foreign Affairs*, Vol. 74, No. 1 (January–February 1995), pp. 26–42.

14. Huntington, "Clash of Civilizations?" pp. 40–41.

15. In *The Other Balkan Wars: A 1913 Carnegie Endowment Inquiry in Retrospect with a New Introduction and Reflections on the Present Conflict by George F. Kennan* (Washington, D.C.: Carnegie Endowment for International Peace, 1993), pp. 11–13.

16. George Schopflin, "Postcommunism: Problems of Democratic Construction," *Daedalus*, Vol. 123, No. 3 (Summer 1994), pp. 137–139.

17. George Schopflin, "Central Europe: Definitions Old and New," in George Schopflin and Nancy Wood, eds., *In Search of Central Europe* (New York: Polity Press, 1989), p. 20.

construct a general picture of post–Cold War Euro-Atlantic security challenges.[18] However, in contrast to the implications of the academic and policy discussions, the media's integration of the democratic peace and civilizational concepts made the perception paradox of Greek security in the post–Cold War alliance system explicit. Indeed, the *New York Times* prophesied as early as spring 1989 that Yugoslavia's "Roman Catholic republics, ... the country's most advanced and politically enlightened region, [would likely face antagonism from a] ... bloc of Orthodox Christian republics."[19] The *Washington Post* commented that "the authoritarian traditions of the dominant Orthodox Church have helped fashion intense nationalism but have not fostered participatory democracy [in southeastern Europe]."[20]

In his popular yet oftentimes historically inaccurate travelogue, *Balkan Ghosts*, Robert Kaplan spoke in terms similar to those of the print media when he argued that "the struggle that pits Catholicism against Orthodoxy, Rome against Constantinople, the legacy of Hapsburg Austria-Hungary against that of Ottoman Turkey,"[21] would mean that, after 1989, "the Cold War and the false division of Europe ... [between] democratic Western Europe and a Communist Eastern Europe ... would now be [replaced by a division between] Europe and the Balkans."[22]

Perception Paradox for Greece: The Integrative Logic of a New Security Strategy

As the main integrative tendencies of the Euro-American security strategy under construction and implementation since 1989, the

---

18. I use the term "media" in the broadest sense to refer to print and electronic media as well as to popular literature.

19. *New York Times*, April 4, 1989.

20. *Washington Post*, February 9, 1990.

21. Robert D. Kaplan, *Balkan Ghosts: A Journey Through History* (New York: St. Martin's Press, 1993), p. 7.

22. Kaplan, *Balkan Ghosts*, p. 48.

democratic peace and the civilizational paradigm raise a fundamental paradox for Greece's role and value in a changing alliance system. The paradox is created by Greece's failure to fit neatly into the integrative logic of the two security concepts. On the one hand, the democratic peace assumes that Euro-American security and a global peace are meant to be the result of an alliance of the market democracies of Europe and America against nondemocratic regimes. On the other hand, the civilizational paradigm characterizes the Orthodox Christian parts of Europe as non-modern, non-democratic, non-Western, and non-capitalist. Integration of the twin concepts of the democratic peace and the civilizational paradigm produces a security strategy whereby enlargement of the alliance community of market democracies would axiomatically exclude those countries in southeastern Europe with an Orthodox religious tradition. For Greece, the integrative logic of the new security strategy is clear: after over four decades of membership in the alliance system and military architectures of the West, and after over two decades of membership in Western political and economic architectures, and after more than two decades of functioning as a pluralist democracy, Greece's Orthodox religious identity suddenly places the country in an opaque security space.

In short, because the integrative logic of the democratic peace and the civilization paradigm suggests that post–Cold War security strategy will give equal weight to cultural and religious variables, on the one hand, and to political, economic, and geostrategic variables, on the other, the Eastern Christian aspects of modern Greek culture have created a perception paradox for Greece *vis-à-vis* its European Union partners and, therefore, have opened up a potentially practical security dilemma *vis-à-vis* its Western alliance cohort.

It bears mentioning that the increasing perception of Greece by its current Western allies in terms that emphasize the country's religious and cultural differences from Europe has been fuelled by a range of factors, relevant and irrelevant to the underlying conceptual tendencies of Euro-American strategy since 1989. Such factors, both cause and effect of the perception paradox of post–Cold War Greek security strategy, include: Athens's policy tilt (real and apparent) towards Belgrade during the war in Bosnia; Greece's inability to match its southern European cohort's effective utilization of structural adjustment funds dispersed under the Delors packages; Brussels's relative indifference to Greek claims in the recent Aegean crisis with Turkey; and Washington's failure to make progress on the Cyprus stalemate, even as the Dayton peace accord brought a technical end to the war in the former Yugoslavia. Significantly, this shortlist of policy cases suggests that Greece's ability to define its role and to protect its interests according to the new rules of the security game may be more than a paradox of perception, indicating instead a more problematic paradox in practical terms. Indeed, a London newspaper succinctly stated that Greece, "from being one of us [Western European] since the War, has become one of them [the Balkans]. With the collapse of the Soviet Empire in eastern and Central Europe, Greece's usefulness [to the Western alliance] ... has disappeared."[23]

Correcting the Perception Paradox & Setting a Security Strategy

Despite the theoretical foundations and practical manifestations of Greece's problematic security status in the post–Cold War era, it would be a mistake to accept that the country's security paradox has become more than one of perception and, therefore, is necessarily a real performance constraint. To support this contention, I will conclude with some specific suggestions about how policymakers in Athens can correct Greece's perception problem and, in the process, set a strategy that identifies Greece's value for Euro-American security objectives while simultaneously maximizing the possibilities for ensuring Greece's specific security interests.

The point of departure is for policymakers in Athens to acknowledge the reality of the country's perception problem and, subsequently, to formulate a corrective response according to the very terms of the democratic peace and the civilizational paradigm. How can this be accomplished? In the most basic sense, policymakers in Athens must begin by explaining to their European and American allies that the categorically successful democratic project underway in Greece over the past two and a half decades has in no way been hindered by the country's Orthodox religious tradition. Indeed, policymakers in Athens should emphasize the fact that Greece's pre-Orthodox, classical history is as relevant to the quality of

---

23. *The Spectator*, March 27, 1994.

democracy in contemporary Greece as is the country's Orthodox, post-classical history. Moreover, policymakers in Greece should point out to members of the Euro-American alliance system that Orthodoxy has in no way compromised Greece's performance as a reliable alliance partner, thereby rendering invalid the assumptions of the civilizational paradigm against Greece's empirical conformity to NATO and WEU models for democracy and likewise suggesting that Orthodoxy has not functioned to differentiate democratic Greece from the tendency wherein democracies rarely wage war on one another.

The above suggestion amounts to Athens's using empirical evidence (that is, Greece's historical reliability as an ally and the country's successful project of democratization since the regime transition in 1974) to make the case that a viable post–Cold War security for Europe and the United States necessarily begins by jettisoning the civilizational paradigm and, instead, concentrating on the promotion of democracy building and transition to market-based economies throughout southeastern Europe. In effect, Greece can correct its perception problem by contributing to the redefinition of post–Cold War security strategy.

In addition to effecting a shift of perception on the part of its allies, Athens can begin to reap the benefits of a post–Cold War Euro-American security strategy focused on democratization and (nonaggressive) marketization only after recognizing that Greece's long-term security interests will be optimally served through the creation of stable democratic regimes and strong economies throughout southeastern Europe and the eastern Mediterranean. This view may require a perception shift on the part of policy-making elites in Athens as well, insofar as such a perspective assumes that Greece is willing to support Turkey's gains along the aforementioned lines.

The shift in perception along the above two axes must be accompanied by practical initiatives on the part of Athens which enhance Greece's credibility as a valued member of the Euro-American security system and, simultaneously, force Athens's allies to invest in symbolic and real terms in Greece's security interests. To this end, Athens could consider concentrating its energies on specific tasks, based on Greece's own successes, associated with promoting market democracies throughout the region.

Three points bear consideration. First, Athens could offer assistance to neighboring countries in the process of democratic transition and consolidation, in improving the constitutional framework, and in implementing the attendant independent judiciary necessary to building the institutional foundations of a pluralist democracy. Second, with regard to particularly sensitive questions of ethnic and religious minority rights, Athens could take the high road in safeguarding the civil rights of its ethnic and religious minority populations along the shared borders with Turkey and the Former Yugoslav Republic of Macedonia. By ensuring the pluralization of politics and society with respect to minority issues, Athens defuses a problem having enormous potential for interstate conflict in the South Balkans and, by the same token, gains credibility with Brussels and Washington regarding constructive allied responses to Athens's calls for the extension of equal rights to Greek and Orthodox minorities throughout the region. Third, Athens could offer to serve as the anchor for regional economic cooperation initiatives, insofar as the Greek economy is the strongest performer in the region; moreover, in the spirit of Stavros Thomadakis's call for collective learning,[24] Athens could explain to its Euro-American economic allies the need to account for the satisfaction of social welfare demands and distributive justice in the process of marketizing the economies of the region, in order to preserve the popular commitment to long-term democratization.

Taken as a whole, Athens's ability to define its security role and to realize its security interests in the post–Cold War era depends upon an immediate corrective response to the paradox of perception which, over the past seven years, has weakened Greece's value in Euro-American strategic planning. The ultimate success or failure of Greece's security performance, however, rests on Athens's ability to recognize the new reality of the post–Cold War security system—wherein security is defined in comprehensive terms, which include military, political, economic, cultural, and natural resource constraints. In this sense, the effective resolution of Greece's nascent security paradox requires the implementation of the equally effective solutions to the multiple gaps between promise and performance that have been explored in this volume.

---

24. See Stavros B. Thomodakis, "The Greek Economy: Performance, Expectations, and Paradoxes," Chapter 3 in this volume.

Perspectives of Policymakers

Chapter 12

Constantine
Stephanopoulos

Issues of Greek Foreign Policy

Greece's policies often seem to bewilder the foreign public who could not possibly be aware of the vicissitudes of a region as complex and complicated as the Balkans. I need not remind you that Greece, as a peninsula situated squarely between Europe and Asia in the eastern Mediterranean, found itself at the center of the course of history. As a result, our country came into contact with numerous peoples and fought long series of battles that sometimes resulted in glorious victories and sometimes in disastrous defeats. In all this interplay of forces and fortunes, the Greek people preserved unabated their national consciousness. They also preserved their language, which, despite the unavoidable evolution it has undergone, remains the same Greek language that has been spoken for thousands of years in our land.

The Greeks, in their dedication to liberty, invented democracy, which they introduced into the history of mankind. However, they were not always able to escape foreign rule, and in the course of centuries, they were subjugated by other peoples. One of these were the Romans, whom the Greeks influenced in a decisive way; another were the Ottomans. It was a great misfortune for the Greek people to fall under their sway at the very moment when the Renaissance was dawning in the West, spurred to a great extent by eminent Greek scholars. This event made it impossible for them to participate as a people in the subsequent cultural development of Europe and plunged them into a long period of darkness relieved only by the links to the West afforded by the flourishing Greek communities to be found in various parts of Europe.

Constantine Stephanopoulos is President of the Republic of Greece.

These remarks were delivered at Harvard University's John F. Kennedy School of Government on October 19, 1995 [editors' note].

Greece emerged as an independent state 165 years ago, bloodied and utterly drained by centuries of enslavement. Once they recovered their political independence, the Greek people turned decisively toward Western Europe and readily assimilated its cultural and scientific gains. In the field of culture and the arts, there arose Greek writers and poets of worldwide distinction, such as Nobel prize winners George Seferis and Odysseus Elytis, as well as other great artists in the field of music, of the cinema, and of the fine arts. Greece's economic development has also been impressive, and our country occupies an honorable place among developed countries.

In order to achieve freedom for the Greek nation, Greece has fought in regional and world wars and has paid for her presence among the democratic nations with blood, toil, and sacrifice. Today, Greece is the only country in the Balkan region with a solidly established democratic regime as well as the only country to be a member of both NATO (joining in 1952), and of the European Union (joining in 1981 as a full member). This renders Greece a factor of stability of great importance to the Balkans. This is all the more so since Greece is one of the few countries in the region not to harbor territorial ambitions against its neighbors. Greece wants to maintain the best possible relations with its neighbors and asks in return only that they respect the rules of international law.

In this spirit, the Greek government has made a determined effort to normalize relations with Albania and is doing its best to remove whatever obstacles might still exist. However, some serious problems remain, owing to reluctance on the Albanian side to allow the large Greek minority living in its southern sector—known to Greeks as Northern Epirus—to fully enjoy the internationally recognized rights of ethnic minorities. The most fundamental of these are the right to be taught in one's own language and the right of religious freedom. Religious freedom involves the recognition and unhindered functioning of the Orthodox Church, to which the Greek minority belongs. Greece, for its part, continues to show its goodwill and the sincerity of its friendly disposition toward Albania by allowing hundreds of thousands of mostly illegal Albanian migrants to stay and work in our country. Their remittances, amounting to $300 million a year, are a fundamental boost to the Albanian economy.

The grave consequences of the collapse of the Federal Socialist Republic of Yugoslavia are a matter of serious concern for Greece.

Given the historical record of the region, it was a mistake on the part of the West to accelerate the breakup of Yugoslavia without first solving some well-known problems. Therefore, it was only to be expected that nationalistic conflicts would ensue. Greece firmly believes that no Balkan or other neighboring country should involve itself in the ongoing conflict, since this would increase the danger of its spread. Accordingly, we have avoided any involvement other than offering objective mediation whenever and wherever it could prove useful. Greece does not support the Serbs at the expense of the Croats or the Muslims. We apportion to each party the responsibility that belongs to it and refuse to accept the notion that any single party is exclusively responsible for the conflict or the war crimes.

The collapse of Yugoslavia had a direct impact on a preexisting problem which had long bedeviled Greece's relations with that country. The problem had to do with the small regional area which in the last fifty years had received the name of Socialist Yugoslav Republic of Macedonia. The situation was aggravated by the dissolution of the Yugoslav federation. It could not therefore be left unsolved any longer without endangering the stability of the whole region. Greece had to act. Some countries were unable to understand the reason for this, owing to their incomplete understanding of the hardships the Balkan people endured and the perils that have threatened Greece since the beginning of the century in that area.

I will not deal with ancient history, as it is needless to dwell on such well-established facts as that the ancient Macedonians were a Greek tribe and Alexander the Great was a Greek, as were his successors Antigonus, Ptolemy, Antipater, and Seleucus, not to mention Cleopatra. It is more useful to remind you of some important events in recent history.

Toward the end of the nineteenth and the beginning of the twentieth century, the region of ancient Macedonia was still ruled by the Ottoman Empire. At the time, the population was mixed, with a clear plurality of Greeks. According to the historical record, there were many Greeks, fewer Bulgarians, even fewer Serbs, Albanians, and Turks. There was no ethnic group called Macedonians.

The impending collapse of the Ottoman Empire prompted a clash between the two major ethnic groups, the Greeks and the Bulgarians, who engaged in a bitter guerrilla war. The Macedonian

Struggle, as this war is known, prevented the realization of Bulgaria's aim to conquer this Greek region but left the Greek population with lasting memories of destruction and suffering. There followed two Balkan wars. In the first Balkan War (1912), Serbia, Montenegro, Bulgaria, and Greece allied themselves against Turkey, expelling it from the greater part of the Balkan peninsula. Bulgaria's ambition to annex the entire Macedonian region was the cause of the second Balkan War, which pitted it against its former allies and was very bloody. Bulgaria lost but did not renounce its aggressive ambitions, and in the two world wars that followed, as an ally of Germany, twice occupied parts of the northern Greek province of Macedonia from 1916 to 1918 and 1941 to 1944. During both of these periods, the local population suffered greatly. After Germany's defeat in both world wars, which entailed also the defeat of Bulgaria, the latter was not in a position to raise any more claims against Greece. Marshal Tito took advantage of this new international situation in order to pursue to his own advantage the same aggressive and expansionist policy against Greece. In 1944, he gave the name of "Macedonia" to that part of Serbia which the latter had acquired as a result of the Balkan Wars, made it into a separate federal republic, and invented a new nationality by naming the population of this republic the "Macedonian people." He also created a new language by dubbing the local idiom "Macedonian language." The newly founded republic was given the name Macedonia in order to constitute the nucleus of a much larger state, which would include in time both the Greek province of Macedonia and the region of Pirin in Bulgaria. The name itself was central to the success of the whole operation, which depended on enlisting the new Macedonian national sentiment and cultivating irredentist feelings.

Greece was not alone in condemning this policy. Then–U.S. Secretary of State Edward Reilly Stettinius, in a letter to American diplomatic missions abroad, pointed out the dangers involved in such a policy and condemned it outright as unfair and unacceptable. However, after Tito broke away from the Soviet Union and made overtures to the West, Western interests dictated that Greece should not engage in too open a quarrel on the Macedonian issue.

Once Yugoslavia collapsed, the former Socialist Yugoslav Republic of Macedonia asked to be recognized as an independent state under the name "Macedonia." As we have seen, this was obviously unacceptable to Greece, since the name Macedonia is a vehicle for irredentist ambitions. These ambitions were also given expression in a constitution that affirmed the existence of a Macedonian people allegedly inhabiting the wider Macedonian area and envisaged its eventual unification. Maps were printed that included within a single Macedonia the northern Greek province of Macedonia. School textbooks were printed presenting a distorted historical viewpoint in order to support these aims. To recognize this republic under the name Macedonia would also have legitimized the usurpation of the historical name and, with it, one of the most glorious chapters in the history of the Greek people. That such fears were not unfounded was soon to be proven by the government of Skopje's decision to include on their flag the emblem of the Macedonian dynasty, discovered in 1977 near the modern Greek town of Vergina.

It should be evident by now that the name Macedonia encapsulates the essence of the policy pursued by the Former Yugoslav Republic of Macedonia at the expense of my country. It should also be readily understandable that if the government of Skopje were to renounce the name of Macedonia, it would renounce at the same time the idea of incorporating the Greek province of Macedonia within its borders. In view of this, Greece had no choice but to react the way it did. Nonetheless, my country, faithful to its peaceful intentions, accepted at the same time the existence of this state. Greece stated that it had no claims against the new state, and only asked that it desist from its expansionist and aggressive policies, and the surest way of doing this was to renounce a name which identifies the state with such policies. This position is reflected in the interim agreement that was recently signed in New York City.

Our relations with Bulgaria and Romania are extremely smooth, and we have developed a close cooperation in many fields. There is growing economic cooperation, and a large number of Greek businesspersons are making significant investments in both countries. This cooperation will receive a major boost from the implementation of various important projects, such as new road links to northern Europe and the construction of a pipeline linking Burgas to Alexadroupolis. Greece has publicly stated that it favors the enlargement of the European Union to include these two Balkan countries in accordance with their stated desire.

Our relations with Bulgaria and Romania constitute an example of good neighborly relations. In fact, there is but one country in the region with whom relations from time to time become dangerously tense, and this country is Turkey. If Turkey were to continue its present policies, it would pose a threat to the stability of the whole region. In Cyprus, Turkey refuses to comply with the United Nations resolutions, and in the Aegean, it insists on putting forth arbitrary claims. You will allow me to dwell a little longer on this point, as it concerns not only Greece but Europe and NATO and, in consequence, also the United States.

Concerning Cyprus, Turkey took advantage in 1974 of the attempted coup against the president of the republic, Archbishop Makarios, to invade Cyprus, purportedly to reestablish the constitutional order. However, once the illegally installed regime collapsed, Turkey not only did not withdraw its troops from the small piece of land it had initially occupied; on the contrary, it undertook a new military operation, this time without any excuse whatsoever, which resulted in the occupation, still in effect, of more than thirty-seven percent of the island. Moreover, in the ethnic cleansing operation in Europe after the second world war, Turkey compelled, in the wake of the military operation, the Greek Cypriot population (some 180,000 people) to flee their ancestral land.

Since that time, Turkey has refused to comply with the resolutions of both the Security Council (353/1974) and the General Assembly that demand the withdrawal of the occupying forces in order to allow the two communities to freely negotiate an internal settlement. Instead, Turkey has installed tens of thousands of settlers from Anatolia in its occupied part of the island in order to alter the demographic ratio, which, on the eve of the invasion, was eighty percent Greek, eighteen percent Turk, with the remaining two percent made up of other ethnic groups, such as the Maronites and the Armenians. On top of all this, in 1983, Turkey prompted the leader of the Turkish-Cypriot community to unilaterally declare an independent "Turkish Republic of Northern Cyprus." The UN Security Council, by resolutions 541/1983 and 550/1984, pronounced this declaration of independence null and void and called upon all member states not to recognize it. To this day, Turkey is the sole country not to comply.

After the fall of the Berlin wall and the reunification of the two Germanies, Cyprus remains the only European state that is still divided by military occupation in defiance of international law. Turkey even goes so far as to invoke the impasse, for which it is responsible, in order to demand that the Republic of Cyprus not be allowed to join the European Union, alleging that this would make any solution of the problem impossible. Logically, however, membership in the European Union should facilitate a solution of the Cyprus problem, since it would provide additional guarantees to the Turkish community and would also help to fill the economic gap that presently separates the two communities.

The stand of Turkey in the Aegean is also manifestly contrary to international law. The Law of the Sea provides that islands are entitled to a continental shelf of their own. Turkey arbitrarily refuses to accept this rule and demands that the continental shelf be divided between Greece and Turkey by drawing a line in the middle of the Aegean as if the innumerable Greek islands did not exist. In order to justify this refusal, Turkey alleges that the Aegean Sea constitutes a special case to which the provisions of the Law of the Sea could not possibly apply, conveniently forgetting that this thesis was put forward in the course of the debates preceding the adoption of the new Convention on the Law of the Sea and was rejected by the conference. If anybody is entitled to invoke the peculiarity of the Aegean, it is Greece, on account of its chain of islands stretching throughout the Aegean Sea.

Utterly different is the attitude of Greece toward international law. Since 1975, Greece has proposed that the two countries have recourse to the International Court of Justice at the Hague for the delimitation of the continental shelf. Souleyman Demirel, who was then prime minister of Turkey, initially accepted this proposal, only to change his mind a few months later.

Since then, Turkey maintains its refusal, even though this proposal is the only way to solve the problem, and insists that the conflict be given a political solution. Turkey aims to bypass the rules of international law and to impose its arbitrary opinions even though they are devoid of any legal or other foundation. It asserts that the implementation of international law would cause it harm. But if you are wronged by the law, this simply means that you are in the wrong.

The situation is similar concerning the question of the territorial waters of Greece. Whereas the Law of the Sea recognizes that every country has the right to extend its territorial waters up to twelve miles, Turkey threatens Greece with war if it were to extend its territorial waters beyond their present six-mile limit. This new, totally illegal demand is based on the assertion that should Greece extend its territorial waters, Turkey will be denied access to the Aegean Sea and will suffocate because of the presence in the Aegean of so many Greek islands. This assertion is utterly false, since it is well known that the Law of the Sea assures everybody the right of innocent passage through territorial waters. This right is extended even to military vessels and submarines. It should moreover be noted that when the provisions of the new Convention on the Law of the Sea were being discussed, Turkey tried and failed to convince the participants to accept its own views on this matter. The threat of Turkey declaring war against Greece is plainly due to the fact that Turkey is well aware that it lacks any valid legal argument to support its position. That is why Turkey resorts to the only principle that might favor it, namely that "might makes right."

This threat was officially expressed in July 1995, in a resolution of the Turkish Grand National Assembly and is backed up by a large number of landing craft stationed on the shores of Asia Minor opposite the Greek islands and is accompanied by declarations of Turkey's military superiority. I feel sincere sorrow that no democratic state has been moved by such a threat to rebuke Turkey and remind it that the UN Charter forbids not only the use of force but also threats of the use of force.

I also feel compelled to mention the behavior of the Turkish authorities toward the Ecumenical Patriarch, who is constantly the target of false allegations by the Turkish press. Turkish authorities have closed the printing press of the Patriarchate and, more importantly, the Theological School of Chalki. This last measure poses a threat to the very survival of the Patriarchate by depriving it of the ability to train new members of the clergy and thus to renew its ranks.

Greece does not engage in any hostile act against Turkey. The assertion that our country actively supports and trains members of the Kurdish Workers Party (PKK) is totally false and, for this very reason, Turkey has been unable to produce a shred of proof in its support. The United States, who is in a position to know, should openly reject these false accusations. It is not the intention nor the policy of Greece to engage in constant disputes with Turkey nor to oppose her legitimate political aims. This is why Greece has accepted the conclusion of a customs union agreement between Turkey and the European Union. If this agreement is in danger of rejection by the European Parliament, this is because of the undemocratic provisions in the Turkish Constitution and the lack of respect of human rights on the part of the Turkish state.

Greece joined the European Economic Community as a full member in 1981 in the belief that only a fully unified Europe will be able to play the global role to which it is entitled on account of its economic and cultural potential. We are all too aware of the obstacles lying in the way of such a goal. National aims are still being pursued at the expense of common European aims, and the diverging interests of member states often come into conflict. Nevertheless, we will continue our endeavor to further the realization of a fully integrated Europe at the Intergovernmental Conference in 1996.

Summing up, I would like to stress once more that Greece wishes to live in peace with all its neighbors. It does not go out of its way to create trouble for any of them. The only thing Greece asks is that neighbors abide by international law and international treaties and conventions. Greece is not prepared to give in to unjust and unreasonable demands and threats. It is my firm belief that the rules of international law and the respect of international conventions should be the sole ways and means of settling international disputes.

Chapter 13

Joseph S. Nye, Jr.

Greece & the Balkans:
A Moment of Opportunity

In Greece long ago, Thucydides explained that honor, fear, and interests are the causes of war. In Greece this century, these three factors often conspired to prevent peaceful relations between the Greeks and their neighbors. In Greece today, an opportunity exists to move beyond ancient animosities and to provide stability and leadership in the Balkans.

The Environment for Opportunity

As Secretary of Defense William Perry explained to Congress last week, the security and stability of Europe is a vital national interest for the United States, and the primary source of European insecurity and instability is in the Balkans. From the beginning of this administration, therefore, we have sought a negotiated settlement to the war in Bosnia. The best chance for peace is now at hand.

It is a sad commentary on the nature of tribal conflicts that it has required more than three years of fighting and dying for the warring parties in Bosnia to begin to recognize the futility of an endless conflict. In the interim, we have seen the rest of formerly Communist central Europe take tremendous strides toward self-sustaining economic growth, institutionalized democratic governance, tolerant inter-ethnic relations, and improved international security. There have been no winners in the Balkan conflict; all the

---

Joseph S. Nye, Jr. is Don K. Price Professor of Public Policy at Harvard University and Dean of the John F. Kennedy School of Government.

These remarks were delivered at Harvard University's John F. Kennedy School of Government on October 23, 1995, in Joseph Nye's capacity as Assistant Secretary of Defense for International Security Affairs, prior to his appointment as Dean of the Kennedy School [editors' note].

parties have lost at least a decade of democratic and economic progress in the senseless pursuit of nationalism and the false security of ethnic exclusivity.

We now believe there is a chance—though definitely not a certainty—for a peace settlement that will ensure a level of security for Muslims, Croats, and Serbs within a Bosnian state. If this agreement is achieved this year, it will be in no small part due to the concerted cooperation of the Contact Group countries and the greater engagement of the United States in the peace process and peace implementation.

We are working hard to bring those peace talks to a soft landing and hope that direct negotiations might begin within a few weeks. For those talks to be successful, we will continue to need the assistance of all interested governments in pressing the parties toward compromise solutions that can ensure a stable peace. Our task is made easier by our knowledge that we can depend on the Greek government to support a settlement and assist us in both political and material ways to secure the peace.

In the process of working toward a peace settlement, however, one quickly realizes that Bosnia is only one piece of a complex puzzle in the Balkans. The interwoven fabric of the former Yugoslavia, while torn by the Croat-Serb and Bosnian conflicts, still exists. As terrible as Bosnia has been, many other misfortunes could emerge in other parts of the former Yugoslavia and surrounding regions.

That recognition forces me to emphasize that the Clinton administration's consistent national security theme of engagement applies directly to the Balkans. We realize that it does little good to resolve the Bosnian conflict if, in the end, we ignore the wider problem of Balkan ultranationalism and ethnic separatism.

Weak democratic processes, nonfunctioning economies, and strong-man militaries only reinforce national insecurities and calls to take up arms. Our policy of engagement, therefore, is designed to affect the sources of insecurity. Part of our approach to a Bosnian peace is to move beyond cease-fires and develop new constitutional principles which will guarantee equitable power-sharing as well as protection of human rights. Moreover, economic reconstruction—especially the rebuilding of intraregional commercial ties across ethnic communities and the joint planning of solutions to postwar economic problems—will be an indispensable ingredient to long-term stability. Finally, greater military transparencies and efforts to stabilize the military balance within Bosnia will reduce misperceptions and hinder miscalculations among the formerly warring parties.

These principles of political engagement, economic reintegration, and military transparency are equally applicable to broader Balkan stability. States neighboring Bosnia similarly will be susceptible to ultranationalism if their economies and democracies falter and if small tensions are allowed to become great tragedies.

Winston Churchill once said that the problem with the Balkans is that the region produces more history than it can consume. While that line is certainly humorous, it is also a bit disingenuous. While ethnic tensions run high in southeastern Europe, I believe that they can be overcome with inspired leadership, or at least managed in order to prevent widespread violence.

At this point in time, the United States is helping provide that leadership in the Balkans. In the years to come, Greece can and must help provide some of that leadership as well.

The Opportunity for Greece

In his paper for this symposium [Chapter 4 in this volume], Monteagle Stearns noted that "as a Balkan and Mediterranean state, and as a member of both NATO and the European Union, Greece is in the best position to provide regional leadership in constructing a Balkan alliance system." And in his paper, Misha Glenny noted that "from the point of view of integration with Western structures, Greece is the most influential state in the Balkans."

I agree with both of these sentiments. No solution providing for stability in the Balkans is attainable without a positive contribution by all Balkan states, especially Greece. Since the disintegration of Yugoslavia, Greece has been victimized by the ensuing conflict as much as any noncombatant; the economic costs of trading and tourism disruptions and the increasing military tensions of the region have imposed a heavy price on Greece. Hence, a stable Balkans will be a great boon for Athens, just as it will be for Sarajevo, Zagreb, and Belgrade. In some respects even more so, since Greece stands to benefit economically more immediately than most other Balkan countries.

But the basis of economic prosperity begins with stable political relations among Balkan partners. During the past three years of the Bosnian conflict, unfortunately, we have witnessed a tendency for nations in the Balkans to expect the worst of others, to revive ancient suspicions, and to isolate rather than engage their neighbors. Thankfully, we also have witnessed signs that this negative trend may be reversing, thanks greatly to Greek leadership. The efforts of the Greek government to improve its relations with the Albanian government have been welcomed, as have the recent agreements reached between Athens and Skopje.

But there are even more opportunities for Greek leadership. Greek leadership is commensurate to Greek power. Like any other nation, Greece possesses two forms of power: hard power and soft power. Hard power is the capacity to force others to do what you want. Soft power is the ability to make others to want what you do. Tyrants rely on hard power, but statesmen are visionary in their use of soft power. While some may concentrate their energies on calculating the regional balance of hard power, Greece has a tremendous advantage over its Balkan neighbors in soft power.

To its Balkan neighbors, Greece is undoubtedly seen as a beacon of strength in a region marked by weakness. Greece's economic vitality and military alliances, its political system and cultural potency, its historical linkages and democratic traditions, all are enviable advantages over its neighbors. Greece's political integration with Western Europe and Greece's economic integration with the global marketplace are bastions of soft power resources. I needn't remind you that Greece, as the only EU member-state bordering other Balkan countries, will carry great influence on states aspiring to eventual EU membership. I need not mention that Greece, as a member of NATO, has a hand on the key to continental security. In all, the Greek moment of opportunity has arrived.

Greek Responsibilities

I don't think it an understatement to say that if Greece adopted a policy of regional leadership, it would have the potential to change the course of the Balkans. In my tenure as Assistant Secretary of Defense, I have had numerous opportunities to speak with Greek governmental officials, both civilian and military, about the Greek-American partnership. I have come away from those meetings impressed by the sincerity of Greek interest in working together to bring peace and prosperity to the Balkans.

But Greek leadership requires Greek responsibilities. It requires us to work together to build the Partnership for Peace and to adapt NATO to suit the new post–Cold War environment. It requires us to work together to speed Balkan economic reconstruction and to reinforce economic cooperation and engagement. It may sometimes require Greece—as the stronger and more secure state—to take the first, sometimes difficult steps to build better relations with its neighbors. It may require Greece to exert efforts domestically to erase old images of longtime adversaries. And it requires Greece to continue to set an example for its neighbors on how to respect democracy and treat minorities.

I began this speech by citing Thucydides. Fear, interests, and honor—these factors start wars. I look forward to future Greek efforts to mitigate ancient Balkan fears and to settle conflicting Balkan interests. I also look forward to a future when Greek honor is never a source of regional tensions, but always a source of regional solutions.

Recalling Thucydides, Greece must work to reduce its neighbors' fears, to recognize its neighbors' interests, and—by doing so—to demonstrate the value of its own honor.

Chapter 14

Michael S. Dukakis

To Be a Greek American

I suspect I came by my interest in politics the way most young Greek Americans did—by being introduced to it by my parents and my aunts and uncles, usually in the form of hot discussions around the dinner table. In fact, I can't remember a time when what was going on politically here in the United States or in Greece or around the world was not a subject of family discussion.

Not that my parents were political activists; they weren't in the usual sense. My dad had come to this country in 1912 at the age of fifteen from the town of Edremit in western Turkey. My mother and her family followed one year later from their home in Larissa when she was nine. Both families settled in old mill cities in the Merrimack Valley of northeastern Massachusetts, and the older sons and daughters went to work immediately in the textile and shoe factories that dotted the New England landscape.

In that sense, they were typical of the thousands and thousands of Greek immigrants who came to the United States in the late nineteenth and early twentieth century. What was different about my parents, however, was that they finished high school and went on to college—a very unusual development among early Greek immigrant families. Both decided to pursue careers in the helping professions—my father as the first American-trained, Greek-speaking doctor in metropolitan Boston; my mother as a school teacher and one of the first young Greek women ever to go to college in New England.

But in our extended family, the fact that you had or had not completed your formal education had little or nothing to do with your interest in politics. If you were Greek, politics was in your blood.

Michael S. Dukakis is former Governor of Massachusetts and Professor of Political Science at Northeastern University.

My mother's oldest brother Nicholas Boukis was a case in point. He came here with his brother Adam before the rest of the family; worked in the shoe factories of Haverhill, Massachusetts; put enough money together to bring the rest of the family over a few years later; and then, with his brother, opened up a small men's clothing store in the shadow of the shoe factories. His formal education ended in elementary school in Greece, but he was a passionate Venizelist, and he bet the family fortune—small though it was—on what he expected would be a smashing Venizélos victory in the plebiscite on the monarchy in 1920.[1] When the Greeks voted in favor of restoring the monarchy, the gloom in my mother's family home could have been cut with a knife; and when my *papou* discovered that Nick had blown the family savings betting on the outcome, there was hell to pay.

Nick was my favorite uncle and my godfather to boot, and I never tired of talking politics with him. He was a bit of a radical when it came to Greek politics, and, in fact, during the 1988 presidential campaign, some of George Bush's operatives began quietly circulating the word that one of my uncles was a Communist. In fact, my uncle Nick was a registered Republican and a devoted supporter of former Republican governor and U.S. Senator Leverett Saltonstall. One of my great regrets is that he never lived to see his nephew become the governor of Massachusetts. He would have been very, very proud.

It is hard to exaggerate the sense of pride that we all had in being Greek. Every Greek boy and girl knew that Athens was the birthplace of democracy, and Greek Independence Day was a major day in our lives. I remember accompanying my dad to a monster Greek Independence Day rally at the Boston Arena when I was only nine and listening to the mellifluous words of Boston's legendary mayor James Michael Curley as he extolled the virtues of Greeks, Greece, and the glories of ancient Athens. And I knew every word of the Greek national anthem that Sunday afternoon in Boston.

We took particular pride in the achievement of young Greeks as they began to make a name for themselves in sports, the professions, and, ultimately, politics. In those days, there were very few

---

1. The Venizelists lost the general election in November 1920. The royalist majority then called for a plebiscite on the monarchy. The king returned to power in December 1920 [editors' note].

Greeks who had won major political offices. In fact, in the Boston area, there was only one—a state representative from the Back Bay section of Boston named George Demeter—and he was a Republican!

But when John Brademas won a seat in the U.S. House of Representatives—an immigrant's son who had graduated from Harvard and won a Rhodes scholarship—we took great pride in his success, and we considered John a role model for the rest of us as we began making our own plans to seek elective office.

There was one other factor that played an important role in my interest in politics and my growing desire to run for elective office, and that was the sense conveyed to me by both of my parents that, as a first-generation American, I had a special responsibility to contribute as much as I could to the country that had welcomed my parents and their families to its shores. "Much has been given to you," they used to say, "and much is expected of you." I'm not sure when I first heard these words that I really understood what my parents were talking about. As I grew and matured, however, it became clearer and clearer. This country had been very good to my parents and their families. "America is the greatest country in the world," my father would say. The implication was clear: we who were lucky enough to be born of immigrant parents in this country owed it a lot—and we should never forget it. That meant working hard, getting an education, taking your responsibilities as a spouse and parent seriously, and being an informed and productive member of the broader community.

My decision to run for office, however, was one that I made without a lot of parental guidance. If the truth be known, I think my father would have felt a lot better, at least at the outset, if I joined a law firm, worked hard, became a partner, and "did well" in the traditional sense of the word. Becoming a professional politician was not something he had ever really contemplated for one of his sons. Not only that, my politics were considerably more liberal than his. In fact, I couldn't get him to register as a Democrat until I started running for office and needed his vote in the Democratic primary. But he was immensely proud of me and what I was doing, and he would have been bursting his buttons with pride, had he lived, to sit in the family box in Atlanta in 1988 when I accepted the Democratic nomination for the presidency of the United States.

It was my mother who was the liberal in the family, and I suspect that's where I got a lot of my political philosophy. She's ninety-two and still going strong and, if anything, more liberal now than she was thirty or forty years ago. Clearly, the Venizelist tradition in the Boukis family lives on!

I first began running for office in the late 1950s. Running as a Greek American in a legislative district in which there might have been a total of fifty Greek families was a fascinating experience. I've always felt that being a Greek American was a real plus in the ethnic politics that played such an important role in the political life of states like Massachusetts thirty or forty years ago. Greeks, after all, were a relatively small ethnic minority. We didn't threaten anybody. And we had done well in the United States. We had a reputation for hard work, family values, a strong commitment to the education of our children, and good citizenship. Every constituent in the town of Brookline whose doorbell I rang had a Greek friend, or had grown up next door to a Greek family, or ate regularly in a Greek-owned restaurant. They liked us, and since so many of them were immigrants or the sons and daughters of immigrants, they felt a common bond with us.

That was particularly true if they had a chance to meet you personally, and I made sure that the Greek work ethic was an important part of my campaigns. We organized ferociously. I climbed stairs and rang doorbells literally every day of the week for six months in my legislative campaigns. My workers and I were up at the crack of dawn, greeting voters at subway and streetcar stops and buttonholing them in front of supermarkets. We didn't mind getting out of bed in the morning and working eighteen hours a day on the campaign—traits that any Greek American and his family can relate to. And people appreciated it.

I also tried to set very high standards of integrity for myself and for the people who worked for me. When in my acceptance speech at the Atlanta convention I included the oath to which young Athenians were expected to swear in ancient Athens, it was not the first time that I had quoted that oath. I first used it when I was inaugurated as governor of Massachusetts for the second time in 1982. And my commitment to those high standards was not simply a function of my love of Greek history. I felt a special responsibility to the Greek community to make sure that I never did anything that would disgrace us or the reputation we had built among our non-Greek neighbors. Spiro Agnew's removal from the office of vice president of the United States for corrupt activities was a terrible blow to the pride of the Greek-American community. I vowed that

I would never let anything like that happen in my case, and although I have made many mistakes in my political career, I don't think anyone has ever questioned my integrity. In that sense, I'd like to think I've been true to the Athenian oath—and to my responsibility to the Greek community as well.

On the other hand, when I first began running for public office, it was absolutely inconceivable, at least in Massachusetts, that a Greek American could ever be elected governor. It just wasn't in the cards. Ethnic politics played too important a role, and there just weren't that many of us.

For that reason, the fact that by 1982 Massachusetts had a Greek-American governor, a Greek-American U.S. senator, and a Greek-American congressman all at the same time was truly remarkable. Paul Tsongas and Nick Mavroules came to their offices in somewhat different ways than I did. But I'd wager that if you asked each of them how and in what ways their Greek heritage played a role, their answers wouldn't differ very much from my own.

In part, our being elected to public office was a wonderful testimonial to the reputation that Greek Americans had made for themselves in their adopted country. In part, it reflected a growing willingness on the part of more and more Americans to put narrow ethnic differences aside and vote for people whom they thought best reflected their ideas and their values.

It just didn't happen to aspiring Greek-American politicians. Before I finished my tenure as governor, I was serving with an Armenian-American speaker of the Massachusetts House of Representatives—itself something that would have been inconceivable in the politics of an earlier generation. Massachusetts voters elected an African American to the United States Senate for two terms; and Boston has recently elected its first Italian-American mayor, although, as I keep reminding him, it probably is because he carries some Greek blood in his veins. After all, we settled southern Italy more than two thousand years ago!

To say that the Greek community responded enthusiastically to my campaigns would be the understatement of the century. They were my earliest supporters. They did so with enormous pride and great excitement. Early in my career as governor, the word got out that my favorite Greek pastry was *diples*. Interestingly enough, my mother, who was a great cook, couldn't make those flaky, honey-covered delights very well, and it was my cousin Olympia's mother, my aunt Alexandra, who would occasionally come over to our house and spend a morning making them.

In any event, my countrymen here in Massachusetts kept me supplied with *diples* for every one of my twelve years as governor. I almost never went on the road as governor without returning with a huge box of them. And this was one gift that I didn't share with my staff. I'd take them home with me and hoard them carefully until I was lucky enough to be presented with the next batch from another outstanding Greek restaurateur and his family.

I did make a serious mistake in my first term, however. Perhaps in an ill-conceived effort to bend over backwards and not play ethnic politics, I did not make a conscious effort to load up my staff and cabinet with Greek Americans, and some Greeks understandably resented it. When I returned to the governor's office four years later in 1982, I didn't make that mistake again. There were plenty of Greek Americans in the administration, and they did a great job for me.

Nothing, however, prepared me for the kind of outpouring that I received from the Greek community when I announced my candidacy for the presidency. It was absolutely overwhelming. Wherever I went, the Greek community was there. In Astoria, Queens, it could take the form of thousands of wildly cheering Greeks on the eve of the New York primary that virtually guaranteed my nomination. In Union, Iowa, it was an unannounced visit to the one pizza place in town, predictably presided over by the only Greek family in the community. In fact, the far-flung network of Greek pizza parlors that covers America were great hosts—and their pizza parlors were the sites of a lot of campaign meetings and receptions for the Dukakis campaign.

My presidential campaign also had the effect of unifying what, as anyone knows who has followed the history of the Greek community in America, has often been a fractious ethnic community. "Every Greek his own prime minister" is not confined to Greece proper. Greeks in the diaspora often carry the same trait with them to their adopted countries, and the history of Greeks in America is a history of both political and religious disputes that continue to this day. All that was forgotten, however, in the Dukakis campaign of 1988. There were a few Greek Republicans for George Bush, but they didn't admit it. And the outpouring of love and support that I received from my fellow Greeks was one of the really extraordinary things about the 1988 presidential campaign. In fact, one of my biggest disappointments in losing was my feeling that I had let down the Greek community. Our primary campaign was picture book perfect and raised the community's expectations to unbelievable heights. Unfortunately, my final campaign was anything but picture perfect, and the letdown in the Greek community was huge. I had promised my fellow Greeks that we'd be dancing the *hasapiko* in the White House, and for a while, we all believed that it was going to happen.

That enthusiasm was not confined to America. Greeks around the world were electrified by the prospect that one of their own might just become the most important political leader in the world. Dukakis bumper stickers and buttons were hot items in Greece. They were also hot items in Melbourne. When I finally left the governor's office at the end of my third term in 1990, Kitty and I were invited to Melbourne for five weeks as guests of the city. Much to my astonishment, I couldn't walk down a Melbourne street without being embraced by a dozen Greek Australians. They knew me, had followed the campaign, and were delighted to see us even in an unofficial role. In fact, one of my fondest memories of our Melbourne trip was a meeting with an eleven-year-old Greek Australian named Michael Dukakis, whose parents had emigrated to Melbourne from Mytilene, the home island of my paternal grandparents. Young Michael had written me a letter during the campaign, and I had answered him, but he was anxious to meet me in person. Kitty and I had a wonderful meeting with him and his family. To make matters even sweeter, the reporter who did the story for one of Melbourne's major television stations was a young woman whose mother was a Dukakis from Mytilene and whose grandfather had emigrated from that island to Shanghai the same year my dad came to America. And none of us were blood relatives!

Being Greek has meant that I have always had an abiding interest in Greece and Greek politics. That interest was whetted by stories of Greek bravery during the Axis invasion of 1940–41 and the unbelievable hardships that the Greek people endured during the Nazi occupation. I was eleven when Stylianos Kyriakidis, the great Greek marathoner, came to Boston in 1946 to run the Boston Marathon and dramatize the plight of the Greek people in a devastated and starving postwar Greece. I remember as if it were yesterday, waiting in Boston's Kenmore Square as the leading runners approached us just two miles short of the finish line and the word came filtering back to us that "it's Kelly and the Greek."

Most of us were torn, because we loved John Kelly, the famed Boston-based marathoner. But when Kyriakidis crossed the finish line in first place with the words "for Greece" on his lips, there wasn't a young Greek American in New England who didn't swell with pride, first because he was Greek and, second, because we knew from our experience during the war that he was doing something important for the land of our parents. He went home with a lot of supplies and a ton of American goodwill.

A year later, President Truman was announcing the Truman Doctrine and involving the United States actively in the Greek Civil War. I'm not sure at that point in my early teens whether I had a particularly good sense of what was going on in Greece, but I certainly knew that the Cold War was upon us and that Greece was one of the first Cold War battlegrounds.

By the time of the Greek junta in 1967, however, I had been serving in the Massachusetts legislature for three terms and had gotten to know many people in the Greek community, a large number of whom were part of a whole new wave of immigrants who had come to the United States after World War II, in many cases to go to school here in the Boston area. They were different from my parents' generation: better educated, politically active, and generally to the left of center in their political orientation. They were passionate about the importance of restoring democracy to Greece after the colonels' takeover, and I became one of their favorite rally speakers, since I shared their outrage over what had happened to the birthplace of democracy. Some of this didn't set very well with older and more conservative Greek Americans, who weren't particularly happy about one of the few Greek-American officeholders in the land being so outspokenly opposed to the junta. But I felt strongly about it, and the colonels' own incompetence and cruelty over time finally brought them down. When millions of Greeks crowded into the center of Athens to welcome Constantine Karamanlis back from Paris with the rhythmic chant *Erhete!* (he is coming!), I felt a kinship with my fellow Greeks who had suffered through the junta that is hard to describe.

Unfortunately, the colonels had more than a little something to do with the effort to oust Archbishop Makarios from his position as president of Cyprus. So, incidentally, did Henry Kissinger. I had met Makarios when he was here in the United States during World War II, and I strongly believed that he was virtually the only public figure in Cyprus who could unite the Greek and Turkish communities. The effort to oust him was not only tragic; it triggered the Turkish invasion of Cyprus and its occupation of a substantial part of that island nation, and we have been trying to undo the damage and the Turkish violation of the most basic tenets of international law ever since. But the role of the colonels in the Cyprus tragedy and their ill-conceived attempt to save their faltering regime with their activities in Cyprus more than justified the opposition of many of us to the junta in the first place. The fact that an American secretary of state had the gall to refer to Makarios as "the Castro of the eastern Mediterranean" rubbed salt in our wounds and has forever made me something less than a fan of Henry Kissinger.

More recently, Greek Americans have had to deal with the even more complicated issue of American policy toward Turkey at a time when Turkey's strategic significance seems limited and its persecution of its Kurdish minority violates all of the values that we say we support. Moreover, the breakup of the former Yugoslavia and the issue of the so-called Republic of Macedonia have required us to get deeply and actively involved in the development of U.S. policy towards Greece and the Balkans.

Personally, I like what I am seeing in the Greek community here in America these days. The so-called "Greek lobby" is a testament to our willingness to get involved and stay involved. There are members of Congress on both sides of the aisle who are working with us. These issues are not only important to us as Greek Americans—they are important to our country, which is in the process of trying to sort out its role in the post–Cold War era and still has a tendency to view things in Cold War terms. Nowhere is this more obvious than in the U.S. attitude toward Turkey, which many old hands in the State Department and some in Congress continue to view as indispensable to our strategic position in the Mediterranean and the Middle East, even though the Cold War is over and the need for Turkey as a buffer against Soviet expansionism has faded into history.

On the other hand, most Americans have little or no knowledge of Balkan and eastern Mediterranean history, and it is exceedingly difficult to try to explain to them, for example, why Greeks have been so exercised over the effort of the people in Skopje to declare themselves a Macedonian republic, use the symbol of Alexander, and draw maps that include large pieces of Greek territory. We have been criticized for it, but I believe it is essential that we organize ourselves in ways that can help our non-Greek colleagues in

Congress and the administration to understand issues that they may have difficulty comprehending without the kind of background and understanding that our heritage gives us. Of course, it also helps to have a Stephanopoulos in the White House. In fact, establishing a tradition of a Greek American on the president's senior staff may be the most important single innovation in American policy making we could possibly advocate!

Through all of this, we need to be in close and constant touch with our colleagues in Greece. Many of us have difficulty understanding the twists and turns of Greek politics. I'm sure many of them occasionally wonder what is going on here in the United States. Keeping in touch. Engaging in constant dialogue. Thinking ahead instead of waiting for crises to hit us. Moving fast to deal with the inevitable crisis that will hit us. These are all important aspects of the kind of ongoing relationship between us that must be encouraged and nurtured.

The recent flap over Turkish claims to Greek territory in the Aegean is a case in point. Once again, American diplomats who didn't understand the situation made unfortunate statements that badly roiled the political waters in Greece. The statements never should have been made. Nevertheless, when it happened, leaders in the Greek-American community immediately got in touch with the White House and members of Congress. Clarifying statements were issued. Much of the controversy that had flared up was defused. The real principle—Turkish observance of the basic rules of international law—was upheld.

In short, whether the issues we are dealing with are profound and of long-range significance or more immediate, the dialogue between Greek Americans in the United States and political leaders and groups in Greece must be strengthened and developed. It is in our best interest as proud heirs of the same political tradition. It is in the best interest of our two countries as well.

Conclusion

Chapter 15

Loukas Tsoukalis

Conclusion: Beyond the Greek Paradox

A short concluding chapter cannot do justice to the wealth of views expressed in this book. It should therefore be seen as another piece of the mosaic, yet also an attempt, however inadequate, to draw out the main theme so that it becomes more clearly defined for the reader. Not everyone is expected to agree with this particular reading of the overall picture; different views are possible and indeed legitimate.

These remarks are intended as a subjective interpretation of the so-called Greek paradox. They are deliberately unbalanced, because the emphasis lies more on the failures than the successes of the last twenty years. The reason is quite simple: the title of the book implies the existence of a gap between promise and performance, and we are invited to offer explanations for it. The title allows no room for complacency, although, of course, it all depends on how promise is defined. But this is a metaphysical question which is left to others to answer.

Diagnosis is supposed to be followed by prescription. In the brave new world of the social sciences, Leninist positivism seems to be legitimized. Can we offer prescriptions for a society as a whole without transforming an analytical piece into a political manifesto? The answer is not at all obvious, but at least the reader has been warned.

Politics Came First

The first observation we can make about the Greek political system in the last twenty years or so concerns the remarkable consolidation

Loukas Tsoukalis is Jean Monnet Professor of European Integration at the University of Athens and Professor and Director of the Economics Department at the College of Europe in Bruges.

164 | THE GREEK PARADOX

of parliamentary democracy. The fact that this is now taken completely for granted is a sure sign of the tremendous progress achieved after the fall of the military dictatorship in 1974. The dictatorship had lasted for seven years and could be regarded as one more episode in the highly unstable history of modern Greek society to that date.

The consolidation of democracy has been accompanied by a major change in the constitutional order, including the abolition of the monarchy and the incorporation of large groups of society into the political system, groups which hitherto had been excluded through a variety of mostly informal measures in the aftermath of the civil war. Consolidation has also been accompanied by a very substantial redistribution of income between different social groups and between city and countryside. The ability of the new democratic system to absorb those changes successfully is an unmistakable sign of its resilience and robustness.

This is the good news. The bad news is that politics has influenced developments in the economic system. To put it bluntly, economic adjustment and international competitiveness were sacrificed for many years on the altar of democratic consolidation. The first important manifestation of resistance to economic adjustment was in the early years of the post-1974 democratic system. Its birth coincided with the first oil shock and the long period of recession which hit all Western economies. The change in the international economic environment brought about the need for difficult economic decisions.

These decisions would have to be about changes in production and consumption patterns. Such changes are always painful and they create losers, at least in the short and medium term, which in politics can be a very long time. Greece's democratically elected leaders tried to postpone this adjustment by resorting to various kinds of protection and subsidization of both producers and consumers. The experience of two other new democracies, namely Portugal and Spain, was remarkably similar at precisely the same time.

But Greece continued to resist adjustment for much longer. The accession to the European Community (EC) in 1981 meant, among other things, the creation of an open economy which would become fully exposed to international competition. The Greek political system and much of Greek society behaved for a long time as if nothing had happened. Uncompetitive firms were artificially preserved for many years, while public budgetary deficits served as a lubricant for the smooth functioning of the political system. As for the welfare state, perhaps overdue by European standards, it was largely built in the 1980s with borrowed money to be paid by future generations. In economics, post-1974 Greece receives very low marks.

Several explanations can be offered for this kind of interaction between politics and economics. One possible explanation has to do with the existence of large sections of Greek society, including powerful and well-organized groups, which apparently had no interest in an open, competitive economy. The relatively closed system, which had survived for many years, had been built on protection and special privileges, the beneficiaries of which would not readily abandon them. This was as much true of those cooing under the protective wings of the state, including most notably the employees of public enterprises, who completely control even now the trade union movement in Greece, as of private entrepreneurs, who operated in the domestic system under arbitrary and nontransparent rules. Many professional classes had also been an integral part of this closed system of privilege, and they had as much interest as any other in resisting real change.

Although Greece is perhaps best known abroad for a significant number of its people, be they entrepreneurs, artists or scientists, who have been extremely successful on the international scene in conditions of strong competition, the situation back home has always been very different. Modern Greek society contains a strong element of dualism, which may offer at least a partial explanation for the so-called Greek paradox.

Social resistance to change and international competition was strengthened by the populist elements of the political system, a populism which had traditionally been closely related to the clientele character of Greek politics. Votes were offered in anticipation of jobs in the public sector and privileged access to finance—through the nationalized banks which still control a very large section of the market—and public services in general. Interestingly enough, populism as a strong feature of political discourse was not weakened with the advent of mass political parties in the post-1974 period. Charismatic leaders and the lack of internal democracy have so far survived the era of mass political parties in Greece.

A low level of economic literacy characterizes the large majority of those dealing with public affairs, be they politicians or journalists. Familiarity with "the dismal science" is not at all common in those circles, where everything tends to be treated as political, preferably with strong ideological undertones. Whether it is day or night is frequently considered a political question rather than a simple matter of fact. This general attitude partly explains how advocates of the so-called developmental dimension of public deficits could be taken seriously for so long. While those deficits persisted in double-digit figures as a percentage of gross domestic product (GDP), public debt soared and growth rates remained consistently below the EC average. Public advocates of economic irresponsibility can be found in all countries, large or small, developed or less developed. The remarkable characteristic of Greece in the 1980s and early 1990s was that they were so many and that they had survived for so long.

The turning point came only a few years ago as the Greek political class became increasingly aware of the unsustainability of large budgetary deficits and the danger of being marginalized as a member of the European Union (EU). Remarkable progress has been achieved since then in terms of macroeconomic stabilization, with a substantial reduction in public deficits (for the first time after many years, the state has been generating primary surpluses), accompanied by a steady decline in inflation rates and interest rates. There have also been growing signs of economic adjustment on the level of individual firms and whole sectors as the armory of non-tariff protection has been progressively dismantled and Greek entrepreneurs have become increasingly conscious of the reality of the open economy, itself a product of EU membership.

The Political Economy of Reform

Given the size of the public debt, which accumulated mostly during the 1980s and now represents approximately 120 percent of GDP, the fiscal consolidation effort needs to continue for much longer. The Maastricht criteria of convergence, which will determine Greece's admission to the final stage of economic and monetary union in the European Union planned for 1999, will help to concentrate the minds of politicians. The criteria will provide an external discipline and also a potential scapegoat for unpopular domestic measures. This is a situation common to several European countries. In the case of Greece, fiscal consolidation is a must, irrespective of Maastricht, unless Greek governments decide to discontinue servicing the debt. And nobody has yet dared to suggest this possibility in public.

Fiscal consolidation would be greatly facilitated if accompanied by a series of structural reforms which are long overdue. They may include the following:

- A reform of the tax system, aimed mostly at a substantial increase in direct tax revenues by widening the tax base. This is particularly important in a country with widespread tax evasion, but it is also very difficult, because of long-established traditions and the high percentage of self-employed (the highest among the OECD countries), who find it easier to avoid paying taxes. Some steps have been taken in this direction, and they have met, not surprisingly, with strong resistance from those directly affected—a kind of revolt by the tax evaders, who represent a very wide spectrum of Greek society, ranging from small shopkeepers to plumbers and lawyers.

- A reform of the social security system, which would have the double aim of introducing effective controls on rapidly rising expenditures, while concentrating more on those in real need. This will become increasingly vital as unemployment rises further and the number of those living below the poverty line grows. An effective social safety net is a necessary precondition for the political viability of the economic adjustment process. And this will inevitably be costly. On the other hand, demographic factors and the small percentage of the population in active employment make the present system unsustainable. The first steps in the direction of reform were taken in the early 1990s. Those who enjoy special privileges under the existing system—generous pensions and early retirement schemes—should be expected to step up their resistance to change.

- A steady reduction in the number of public employees, which is excessive by any international standard. Greece is a state with strong signs of elephantiasis; it is too big and unable to move at all flexibly. Fewer civil servants, better paid, with a minimum degree of meritocracy in terms of appointments and promotions, should be the goal of a much broader exercise of administrative reform aimed at cheaper and better services for the citizen. Administrative reform has figured prominently in the political agenda for many years, but with very little tangible effect so far. It is supposed to be very costly, in the way politicians measure cost.

- The introduction of modern management techniques in the public sector, especially hospitals and public enterprises. Inefficiency, coupled with corruption, leads to an enormous waste of public resources. Pressure from Brussels acts in this respect as an important catalyst for change. In the area of public procurement, for example, some degree of rationalization and transparency is a necessary precondition to the continued flow of EU money through the Structural Funds.

In many cases, efficient management may be totally incompatible with state control, unless the state were to be reformed beyond recognition, which certainly will not happen tomorrow. Greece has not yet followed the majority of European countries in large-scale privatization of state-controlled enterprises. In recent years, there has been some selling off or closing down of private-sector lame ducks which had been taken over by the state during the 1980s in a short-sighted attempt to prevent an increase in unemployment. The "old family silver" still remains untouched, however, even though its state owners seem remarkably unable to preserve it in good condition, while consumers and taxpayers are charged high prices to pay the salaries of those who take poor care of it.

These cases represent the kind of structural reforms needed as part of a radical overhaul of the state machine, an overhaul which is long overdue and not only for economic reasons. Greece needs a smaller and more efficient and flexible state organization that leaves enough room for civil society to grow, while also shifting its role from the direct control of production to the regulation of economic activity. This is a big challenge whose implementation will extend well beyond the end of this century.

The reformist agenda in Greece is indeed very long and the obvious question to ask is what kind of political coalition can successfully run with it. Some useful lessons may be drawn from the experience of recent years. The first is that the political forces in favor of reform cut right across the two main parties in Greece. The second is that those forces have remained small in number for a long time when compared with countries on a similar level of political and economic development, such as Spain and Portugal. The encouraging sign is that those numbers have been steadily growing, especially among the professionals and the better educated. The election of Kostas Simitis to the post of prime minister in January 1996 may suggest that the reformists have now gained the upper hand, although it still remains to be seen whether this election signifies a more permanent shift in the internal balance of force in PASOK and in Greek society in general. The third lesson is that membership in the European Union generally acts as a catalyst for reform, with budgetary transfers from Brussels sometimes breathing extra life into antiquated structures of the recipient country.

Whether political and economic reform will necessitate a major realignment of political forces in Greece or whether it can be undertaken by the existing political formations, separately or in grand coalitions, is still impossible to assess. Only time will tell. The most crucial imperative is that the process of real reform begins soon and that it gains its own momentum. Who delivers the goods is less important.

In a country where politics has traditionally been about anything and everything, civil society has remained underdeveloped. The quality of democracy in Greece largely depends on the strengthening of independent groups and associations of citizens which can act as effective controls on the all-expansive and occasionally authoritarian tendencies of the state. In recent years, there have been some encouraging signs in this direction, although much more needs to happen.

Foreign Policy: Defending Interests or Rights?

Since 1989, the European political map has changed beyond recognition and the countries of the old continent are still adjusting to the new realities of the post–Cold War era. Long-established totalitarian regimes collapsed like a house of cards, and only a few years later, the old communist parties, under a variety of newly acquired names, were returned to power through democratic processes to pursue programs of economic reform. The transition to parliamentary democracy and a market economy has proved long and painful. State institutions have also suffered from the strong winds of change. Countries have broken up, some peacefully, others with blood and tears.

The North Atlantic Treaty Organization (NATO) and the European Union now constitute the bright objects of desire for virtually every country of Central and Eastern Europe, and this desire may not be satisfied for several more years. NATO worries about the implications of granting security guarantees to countries paralleling the long Russian border (and the threatening voices coming from Moscow make this prospect even more difficult), while the European Union tries to measure the cost of adding more members, this cost being measured in both institutional and policy terms. The parameters of the new political order in Europe have not yet been clearly defined.

Greece finds itself in a very unstable neighborhood, a neighborhood which has suffered a great deal from the long and bloody war in the former Yugoslavia, which sometimes threatened to ignite the old sparks of ethnic hatred in the Balkans. Greece's political leadership and the country as a whole were caught unprepared and they proved unable to play an effective stabilizing role in the area.

The balance sheet of Greece's policy in the Balkans since the collapse of communist regimes is not very positive, although it has been rapidly improving since a decision was made to settle bilateral disputes with its northern neighbors through negotiations. Arguably, external powers have committed much bigger mistakes, especially during the early stages of the disintegration of Yugoslavia. But this can hardly serve as a consolation for a small and vulnerable country like Greece whose diplomatic mistakes have sometimes carried a very heavy price.

Because of the level of its economic development, the stability of its democratic institutions, the homogeneous nature of its population—not to mention its access to international high-society clubs(!) such as the European Union and NATO—Greece is in a privileged position *vis-à-vis* the other countries of the region. If anything, one might have expected Greek policies to exude an excessive degree of confidence. In reality, however, things have been very different. Greek official attitudes have been reactive and almost entirely defensive.

The collapse of the old communist order in the north has presented Greece with both opportunities and risks, ranging from the opening of an economic hinterland to the explosion of old ethnic rivalries. Private entrepreneurs have concentrated on the opportunities, while official Greece, including the large majority of the political class and the mass media, has focused almost exclusively on the risks. For several years, Greek foreign policy exhibited a rather peculiar combination: defensiveness and a strong sense of insecurity, coupled with a tendency to open up too many fronts, which might have been interpreted as a sign of strength if it were not simply the product of poor judgment. Greek policy was characterized by a clear lack of strategy and an inability to establish priorities.

There was a time in the early 1990s when Greece had serious bilateral disputes with both Albania and the Former Yugoslav Republic of Macedonia (as it is still officially known) not to mention with Turkey, constantly a figure on Greece's agenda of problems. Open bilateral disputes were combined with an unprecedented degree of isolation of Greece from its European partners and NATO allies, an isolation that even powerful countries can ill afford.

Greece's official message transmitted to the world at large was extremely unclear; it was highly emotional and it referred repeatedly to rights not immediately recognizable by foreigners. To make matters worse, the message was delivered in a language that hardly anyone else abroad could understand.

The pathology of Greek foreign policy perhaps could be summarized in the following terms. It all starts with a strong sense of insecurity, which sometimes turns into a siege mentality, in a country that is, admittedly, surrounded by difficult neighbors who may easily turn into enemies (they have often done so in the fairly recent past), ready to challenge the status quo. This is particularly true of Greece's relations with Turkey, which Greeks perceive as a major external threat.

This sense of insecurity, which is certainly not created out of nothing, is cultivated by a sensationalist press and other mass media, while most members of the Greek political class appear only too ready to dance to the populist tune. Political discourse emphasizes Greek rights, which are thought to extend back to ancient times, rather than Greek interests, which require defense using arguments and intelligent diplomacy. Greece's version of political discourse has not proved to be an exportable commodity.

Greek references to their rights, rather than their interests, also make negotiations and the bilateral give-and-take with foreigners more difficult to accept by the wider public. A highly moralistic language is used, which frequently leads to rejectionist attitudes by

Greeks if foreigners fail to respond appropriately. On the other hand, it is perhaps fair to add that Greece's partners and allies, motivated by a strong (and misconceived?) sense of *realpolitik*, have so far done very little indeed to calm Greek fears about the perceived threat from the east.

As with economic policy, Greece's political class took some time to recognize that foreign policy had reached a dead end. With this realization and active prodding from Western capitals, most notably Washington, significant steps have been taken since then towards improving bilateral relations with northern neighbors. A minimum degree of consensus has begun to emerge among the major political parties on Greece's Balkan policy.

The further strengthening of consensus on foreign policy issues and a more dispassionate and clear-headed approach to international affairs would benefit a great deal from the functioning of independent organizations and institutes. Their main task should be the dissemination of information, the promotion of internal dialogue, and the establishment of multiple channels of communication with the rest of the world. Existing organizations and institutes are still rather weak, and this weakness usually has financial roots. As with other policy areas, foreign policy could benefit by access to sources of information and analysis that are not under the exclusive control of professional politicians. This is another manifestation of civil society which is in need of encouragement and support.

Relations with the still-unmentionable republic in the north will require a great deal of care and sensitivity from both sides. The problems associated with the birth of an independent republic out of the old Socialist Yugoslav Republic of Macedonia were not simply a figment of Greek imagination. It was seen as a source of irredentism and political instability. The analysis being arguably correct, it led, however, to the wrong policy conclusions. For several years, Greece behaved as if a return to the old Yugoslav status quo were indeed possible or as if irredentism could be baptized away. Potential dangers were exaggerated, windows of opportunity were repeatedly closed, and relations between Athens and Skopje progressively deteriorated.

Greece now recognizes the necessity, if not the desirability, of an independent state consisting mostly of Slav Macedonians and Albanians on its northern border. Some may refer to it as a buffer state, but this is not necessarily a pejorative term. Greece has every interest, and also the capacity, to contribute to the political stability and economic prosperity of this new country. But because of old wounds—after all, Greece's civil war and the role played by Slav Macedonians in it are still vividly remembered by the older generation in Greece—bilateral relations need to be handled with great care by both sides. A very important measure of confidence building would be a compromise on a (composite?) name for the new republic. Notions of exclusivity and monopoly are indeed very dangerous for the region.

Relations with Turkey are much more difficult and potentially explosive. In political and military terms, Greece is the weaker party that refuses to negotiate under duress, emphasizing instead international rules and arbitration procedures. Even though foreign powers could play a constructive role, it needs to be understood that the solution to bilateral problems with Turkey cannot be imported from outside. Greece requires a long-term strategy in its relations with Turkey. It needs to explore those issues on which it can have a constructive dialogue with the other side and also to explore and develop multiple channels of communication with individuals, groups, and political parties who may also have an interest in communicating with Greeks.

Turkey is, of course, not a monolithic society, and Greece has a strong interest in a European (and Western) Turkey. Having said that, we might also add that the dilemma often presented to Greece by its Western allies—namely, a Turkey that either retains a privileged (and pampered) relationship with the West or falls victim to Islamic fundamentalism—is rather crude. It does no justice at all to the complexity of Turkish society, its political institutions, and the kind of model of economic development adopted.

There is, however, a fundamental question that needs to be answered. Given the existing political balance of forces, is Turkey a status quo country? And if the answer is no, what, if anything, do EU partners and NATO allies propose to do about it? Would they be prepared to tolerate a revisionist policy with all the negative implications that such a policy would have for peace in the region? Greece's behavior inside European and transatlantic organizations very much depends on the answer.

Our final point refers to the European and Atlantic dimension of Greece's foreign policy. Greece is (thank God!) a member of the European Union. This means that economic, political, and institutional developments in the country have been and will continue to be influenced decisively by its membership in the Union. The security dimension has, of course, been largely determined by Greece's membership in NATO, an organization in which the United States has always been more than a *primus inter pares*. Recent developments in the Balkans have, if anything, strengthened the American presence in the region.

A stronger and more unified European Union (which might prove to be only wishful thinking for the next few years) will strive to develop the defense dimension of European integration by internalizing and further extending the functions of the Western European Union (WEU). This would be only natural for a political unit with federalist aspirations. The strengthening of the European Union and of the European defense arm should not, however, be seen as incompatible with the preservation of strong transatlantic ties and a continued U.S. presence in Europe. Greece should strive for both, and it should always avoid being placed in a position of having to make a choice between the two.

Index

Center for Science and International Affairs

Graham T. Allison, Director

John F. Kennedy School of Government, Harvard University

79 JFK Street, Cambridge MA 02138   *(617) 495-1400*

The Center for Science and International Affairs (CSIA) is the hub of research and teaching on international relations at Harvard's John F. Kennedy School of Government. CSIA seeks to advance the understanding of international security and environmental problems with special emphasis on the role of science and technology in the analysis and design of public policy. The Center seeks to anticipate emerging international problems, identify practical solutions, and encourage policymakers to act. These goals animate work in each of the Center's four major programs:

- The International Security Program (ISP) is the home of the Center's core concern with international security issues.

- The Strengthening Democratic Institutions (SDI) project works to catalyze international support for political and economic transformations in the former Soviet Union.

- The Science, Technology, and Public Policy (STPP) program emphasizes public policy issues in which understanding of science, technology, and systems of innovation are crucial.

- The Environment and Natural Resources Program (ENRP) is the locus of interdisciplinary research on environmental policy issues.

Each year CSIA hosts a multinational group of approximately 25 scholars from the social, behavioral, and natural sciences. Dozens of Harvard faculty members and adjunct research fellows from the greater Boston area also participate in CSIA activities. CSIA also sponsors seminars and conferences, many open to the public; maintains a substantial specialized library; and publishes a monograph series and discussion papers. The Center's International Security Program, directed by Steven E. Miller, publishes the CSIA Studies in International Security, and sponsors and edits the quarterly journal *International Security*.

The Center is supported by an endowment established with funds from the Ford Foundation and Harvard University, by foundation grants, by individual gifts, and by occasional government contracts.

DATE DUE